Living in

the

United States

by Raymond C. Clark,
and Arthur A. Burrows

Tenth Revised Edition

PRO LINGUA ⬤ ASSOCIATES

Pro Lingua Associates
P.O. Box 1348
Brattleboro, Vermont 05302 USA
Webstore: www.ProLinguaAssociates.com
802-257-7779   Orders: 800-366-4775
Orders@ProLinguaAssociates.com
SAN 216-0579

ISBN 10: 0-86647-374-2, 13: 978-0-86647-374-3

This book was originally developed by The Experiment in International Living, Brattleboro, Vermont, as part of its Orientation Development Project. The initial development funds were provided by the U.S. Information Agency under the President's International Youth Exchange Initiative.

The staff of the original development project were: Ani Hawkinson, writer; Alvino Fantini, director; Julie Soquet, project and orientation director; Joy Wallens, production.

Peter deJong, former Secretary General, and the Directors of the various Experiment in International Living National Offices identified the original content areas covered in this country-specific series.

Since the second edition, the writers and editors have been Raymond C. Clark and Arthur A. Burrows. Many revisions and additions made in the fourth and later editions were suggested by David P. Rein and Edgar Sather.

Designed and set by Arthur A. Burrows using Palatino text and Monotype Corsiva display types. Photos from the Dreamstime.com Agency: front cover © Nruboc, back © Tsung-heng Chen (SF), © Pmudu (Y), © Elyssa Conley (NH), p i © Anthony Aneese Totah, Jr., p vi © Jruffa , p 7 © Erwin Purnomo, p 13 © Yao Meng Peng, p 19 © Ron Chapple Studios, p 20 © Gary Beet, p 27 © Edyta Powwlawska, p 30 © Mehmed Dilsiz, p 31 © Zhudifeng, p 37 © Anne9001, p 62 © Lisa F. Young, p 64 © Rmarmion.

Cover design by Arthur A. Burrows.
Printed by Royal Palm Press in Punta Gorda, Florida.

Tenth, revised edition for 2015
Printed in the United States of America

iv

U.S. Capitol, Washington, D.C.

Living in the United States

The first Thanksgiving

O beautiful for spacious skies,
For amber waves of grain,
For purple mountain majesties
Above the fruited plain!
America! America!
God shed his grace on thee
And crown thy good with brotherhood
From sea to shining sea!

Katharine Lee Bates, 1893

Contents

3. Country Facts   42

Jefferson Memorial

Appendix: The 50 States   69

Special Note

In this book we have used the terms *America* and *American* to mean "the United States" and "citizen of the United States." We are aware that people from the other Americas are also Americans. Unfortunately there are no other single words in the English language at this time that can be used in place of "America(n)."

1. Basic Information

This section of the book is about the basic and general facts about living in the United States. However, every state, city, and town will be a little different. You will need to find the differences and the details. For example, we can tell you about restaurants in the United States, but you must find the places that have food that you like. We can make suggestions, but you need to make the final choices. Good luck!

1.1 Money and Banks

The **dollar** is the currency of the United States. There are 100 cents in a dollar. American money comes in the following denominations: 1, 5, 10, 25, 50-cent, and one-dollar coins and 1, 2, 5, 10, 20, 50, and 100-dollar bills (paper money). The 50-cent and dollar coins and the $2 bill are not common.

Paper Money. American paper money is all the same size and printed on the same color paper, but there are small differences in the color of the printing. They have recently been redesigned, so you may find two different designs for any bill. The coins also vary. There are many different quarters (one for each state and several featuring beautiful natural sites). There is a dollar for each president, and five Jefferson nickels.

Coins. American coins have special names which you need to know.

1 cent	— a penny
5 cents	— a nickel
10 cents	— a dime
25 cents	— a quarter
50 cents	— a half-dollar

Carry some change (coins) because you may need exact change for certain services, such as parking meters, telephones, and buses (see sections 1.6, 1.8, and 1.9). You may also find that large bills ($50, $100) are not accepted at small stores.

You should not carry a large amount of cash. Bring an internationally recognized credit card. They are acceptable almost everywhere.

Credit/Debit Cards. Nowadays people use credit cards or debit cards for many of their purchases. You make a payment on your credit card every month. A debit card is connected to your bank account. When you use your debit card, the money is withdrawn from your bank account immediately. MasterCard and Visa are the most widely accepted credit cards. To rent a car you need a credit card. Most hotels require a credit card when you call to make a reservation and when you check in.

Changing Currencies. If you bring a commonly used international currency with you, you may change it at a large international airport. You can also change it at a bank, but it is not always easy to change international currencies at banks in small towns. It is usually better to bring dollars with you. When you arrive at an international airport such as JFK in New York, you may need one-dollar ($1) bills to rent a baggage cart. Porters are not available before you clear customs, so you must carry your own baggage.

Banks in the United States tend to be local and regional. For example, Citibank is one of the largest American banks, but it does not have branches throughout the United States. For this reason, a checking account with a local bank is not useful outside your hometown — except for paying by mail. However, if you are going to stay in one place for a month or more, you may want to open an account at a local bank. It is very easy to do.

Banks are usually open from 9:00 a.m. to 5:00 p.m. and on Friday until 6:00 P.M. They are not open on holidays (see section 2.14) or Sundays; some are open on Saturdays.

Most banks offer savings and checking accounts. There is usually a fee for checking accounts. With most banks, you can check your account balance and pay bills using the bank's web site. Banks also offer the **ATM** (Automatic Teller Machine) service. With your ATM card you can deposit and withdraw money at an ATM any time. You can use ATMs all over the country. There are fees for this service.

1.2 Food

Americans usually eat three meals a day — breakfast, lunch, and dinner (see section 2.11). Certain kinds of food are typical at each meal. Throughout the United States, the food is similar, but there are some regional differences. In general, American food is plain and not spicy.

The Burger. One of the most popular American foods is the burger. Hamburgers are made of beef, not ham. They are served in a round piece of bread called a bun. They are often eaten with one or more of the following: tomato, lettuce, onion, mustard, and ketchup. A hamburger with melted cheese on top is called a cheeseburger. Some restaurants have other kinds of burgers with other names, such as "jumbo burger" (very big), "bacon burger," "mushroom burger," "veggie burger," or "turkey burger." If the menu doesn't explain the different kinds of burgers, ask the waiter for help.

Hot dogs (also called "franks" or "frankfurters") are a kind of sausage. They can be steamed, boiled, or grilled. They are served in a long bun with mustard or ketchup or pickle relish. Hot dogs are often made from pork — the meat from pigs. (Bacon and ham are also meat from pigs.) If you want to avoid pork, all-beef and turkey hot dogs are generally available.

Sandwiches. Americans eat a lot of sandwiches — especially for lunch. They are made with two pieces of bread and a filling. Some common fillings are tuna fish, egg salad, ham, chicken, turkey, roast beef, cheese, and peanut butter and jelly. Some sandwiches are hot — for example, a hot roast beef sandwich. Another special type is the club sandwich, which is made with three pieces of bread and two fillings between the three pieces. The fillings are often chicken or turkey and ham with lettuce and tomato. Sandwiches made with pita bread are called pockets or wraps. Sandwiches made with a long, round bread are called grinders, subs (submarines), hoagies, or heros. They are very popular.

Pizza is another food eaten in all parts of the country. A large, flat piece of bread is typically covered with tomato sauce and cheese and then baked. Pieces of meat and vegetables are often sprinkled on top of the cheese.

Main Dishes. For main dishes – especially for dinner – Americans eat a lot of red meat. Nowadays, people are eating more fish and poultry than they used to. Beef is the most popular meat, followed by pork and lamb. In a few places you can find rabbit meat, but you will not find horse, goat, or dog meat. There are many kinds of beef. Hamburger (ground beef) and beef steak are the most common. In general, Americans like thick steaks. There are three ways to cook meat: rare (not cooked very much), medium, and well done (cooked a lot).

Pasta is popular all over America. Spaghetti with a tomato sauce is often a main dish. Noodles of many kinds are served as side dishes. Macaroni and cheese is very popular.

Salads are often served with a meal. They are eaten before or with the main dish. A salad can also be a main dish — especially for lunch. There are many kinds of salad, but some of the most common ingredients are lettuce, tomato, onion, and cucumber. A kind of sauce called a salad dressing is poured on the salad. There are many different kinds of dressings, but the most common types are Italian (oil, vinegar, spices, and herbs), Thousand Island (mayonnaise, ketchup), French (oil, vinegar, mustard, tomato), and blue cheese. Some restaurants have their own dressing, which is called the house dressing. Many restaurants offer a chef's salad. It is a large salad – a full meal. In addition to vegetables, it usually contains small pieces of chicken, turkey, ham, and cheese. One other kind of salad, made from cabbage and served in a creamy dressing, is called cole slaw.

The Potato. America's favorite vegetable is the potato. It is served in many different ways. The most common are baked potato (a whole potato cooked in an oven), mashed potatoes (boiled potatoes mixed with milk and mashed into a puree), French fries, and potato chips (strips and slices of potato fried in a deep pot of oil). In a restaurant, you may be asked to choose which kind you want (see section 1.3).

Corn is a truly American vegetable (it can also be called a grain, like wheat and rice). It was grown by Native Americans before the Europeans came to the Americas. Canned or frozen corn can be found all year, but fresh corn is eaten in the summer (July and

August). It is especially popular to eat the kernels of corn off the whole ear (cob) while holding the ends with your fingers. This is called "corn on the cob."

Starches. Pasta, bread, potatoes, and corn are all starches. Americans generally eat some meat, a starch, and green or yellow vegetables at dinner. They may eat a green salad or a hot vegetable. Popular vegetables found throughout the United States are peas, beans, carrots, lima beans, broccoli, cauliflower, Brussels sprouts, squash, spinach, and cabbage. Other vegetables are popular regionally. In general, most vegetables are boiled. In recent years many Americans are finding new ways to prepare and serve vegetables – steaming and stirfrying, for example. Many people have decided to become vegetarians, meaning they do not eat meat. Vegans do not eat meat or dairy products.

Breakfast. For breakfast, some Americans eat only bread, some kind of fruit (most often orange juice), and coffee or tea. The bread is usually heated and is called toast. Another kind of breakfast bread is the donut (also spelled "doughnut"), a sweet, round piece of fried bread with a hole in the middle or a filling. Another kind of bread often eaten at breakfast is the bagel. It looks like a donut, but it is not sweet; it is first cooked in water and then baked in an oven. Some shops specialize in donuts or bagels.

Cereal. Many Americans eat hot or cold cereal for a quick breakfast. Cereals are made from wheat, oats, rice, or corn, and there are many different kinds. Cold cereals that are brightly colored and sweetened are especially popular with children. Cereal producers spend millions of dollars to persuade children and parents that their cereal is exciting and tasty. People serve cereal with milk and sometimes fruit.

Pancakes, etc. When Americans take the time for a bigger breakfast, they often eat eggs (fried, boiled, or scrambled) with bacon, sausage, or ham. Pancakes, waffles, and French toast (bread soaked in egg and milk and then fried) are also popular for bigger breakfasts. They are generally served with a sweet syrup, often maple flavored.

Snacks. Americans also eat between meals. These foods are called snacks. Most snacks are not very nutritious. Chocolate and other candies, potato and corn tortilla chips, crackers, pretzels, and popcorn, and cookies and sweet pastry are all very common. This kind of food is called "junk food."

5

Fast Food. The fast food industry has had an important influence on what and how Americans eat. McDonald's is the leader in this industry. It is now known throughout the world. McDonald's has made the American hamburger famous. One reason is that in every McDonald's the food is exactly the same and is cooked in exactly the same way. In addition to the nationally known burger chains (McDonald's, Burger King, and Wendy's), other famous fast food restaurants specialize in chicken (KFC), Mexican food (Taco Bell), donuts (Dunkin' Donuts), and pizza (Pizza Hut, Domino's, Little Caesar's).

Local Options. Although the fast food industry has restaurants in every American town, there are also local and regional differences in American food that you should look for wherever you live or travel. The differences and specialties are too numerous to mention in this small book, but you can find them. Ask, look, and explore.

1.3 Restaurants

Family Restaurants. Fast food restaurants are the same everywhere in the United States. Local restaurants offer more variety. Here are some general types to look for. Family restaurants are good places to bring children. The food is not very expensive and is probably typically middle-class American. These restaurants may not serve alcohol, so if you like a glass of wine or beer with your meal, ask before you sit down (see section 1.4).

Cafeterias. In cafeterias you walk through a line, choose your food, put it on a tray, pay at the end of the line, and carry your food to an empty table. The food is usually inexpensive, and it is ready to eat. Cafeterias are commonly found at schools.

Other informal places to eat are called cafes, coffee shops, sandwich shops, delis (a kind of sandwich shop), diners, and truck stops. While driving along America's highways, you may find it interesting to stop at a truck stop and listen to the conversations of the long-distance truck drivers.

Steak houses and seafood restaurants are often more formal and expensive, but they are very common.

Here are a few things you should know about American restaurants:

- Most restaurants do not allow smoking. This varies in different cities and states. Ask before you smoke.
- Many restaurants post menus in the window so you can see the prices before you enter. If they do not, it is acceptable to enter the restaurant and ask for a menu before you sit down, If it is too expensive, it is OK to leave.
- At many restaurants, lunch is less expensive than dinner.
- You can often save money on breakfast by ordering "specials."
- Bread and butter and water are usually served free with the meal.
- If you do not eat all your food you may ask for a "doggie bag." The waiter will put your uneaten food in a bag, and you can take it home.
- To ask for the check, signal the waiter with your eyes or a raised hand. If that doesn't work, you can say, *"Excuse me,"* quietly when the waiter comes near you. Then say, *"May we have the check, please?"*
- The charge for service, called "the tip," is usually not included in your restaurant bill, usually called "the check." You may ask if the tip is included.
- You must calculate the tip. The normal amount is 15% to 20%. If the service is poor, you may leave less. Waiters are usually paid a low wage, and they need their tips to live on.

7

- There is usually a meals tax added to your restaurant bill. The amount varies from state to state.
- Waiters or servers will be both men and women.
- In some restaurants, waiters have helpers called bus boys. They set tables, bring bread and water, and clear away used plates, but they cannot take orders.

Restaurant Customs. It is common in the United States to find a sign saying "PLEASE WAIT TO BE SEATED" when you enter a restaurant. This means you have to wait near the sign. Someone will come to show you to your seat. The wait is usually not very long. If the restaurant is crowded, you may be told there will be a wait. They will ask for your name. Then you will be called by name when there is a place for you. Before giving your name, ask how long the wait will be. You don't have to stay. If the restaurant is not crowded, you may see a sign that says, "PLEASE SEAT YOURSELF."

In restaurants, you should be prepared to answer some questions. Here is a list:

- *How many in your party (group)?*
- *Would you like something to drink before you order?*
- (At breakfast) *How do you want your eggs? (soft-boiled, scrambled, poached, fried either sunny-side-up or over-easy, or in an omelet)*
- *What kind of toast do you want? (white, wheat, or rye)*
- *What kind of dressing do you want (for your salad)?* (see section 1.2)
- *How do you want your steak? (rare, medium, or well done)*
- *Baked, mashed, or fries? (potato)*
- *Would you like some dessert?*
- *Regular or decaf (coffee)?*
- *Do you want your coffee black or with cream and sugar?*
- (In fast food restaurants) *Is that for here or to go?*
- *How's everything? Is everything all right?* (Waiters usually ask this to see if you need anything and if your food is OK.)
- *How is everything? Are you still working on it?* (Are you still eating?)

8

Ethnic Restaurants. In large cities you can find a wide variety of ethnic restaurants. In small towns you may also find some special ethnic restaurants, depending on the nature of the local population. If there are Thais or Polish people in the community, you may find a Thai or Polish restaurant. All over the United States, from big cities to small towns, you will find Chinese, Italian, and Mexican restaurants. Indian, Japanese, French, and German are also common in some parts of the country.

Counters and Bars. Some restaurants have a counter at which customers can sit and eat. Many other restaurants have a bar at which customers can sit while drinking alcohol. There are almost always bottles of alcohol on shelves on the wall behind the bartender at a bar. Often it is possible to get food with alcohol at a bar. Children may always sit at a counter where only food is served, but in most of the country it is not appropriate for children to sit at a bar. Some places specialize in serving locally made beer (craft beer). These may be called breweries, pubs, or brewpubs, and yet they are appropriate for children who sit with adults at a table. However, bars, pubs, or breweries which are mostly for drinking alcohol will usually not allow children to enter, and women who are alone may want to avoid them.

1.4 Drinking and Smoking Laws

Driving Laws. There is a law in the United States that prohibits people under the age of 21 from drinking or buying any alcoholic beverage ("drink"). When you buy or order an alcoholic drink, you may be asked to show proof of your age. You must be 21 or over. You will need a photo-ID (identification card), such as a passport or a driver's license. You will not be allowed in bars and discotheques if you are under 21. You may be stopped at the entrance and asked to show your ID. Bar owners can lose their license to serve alcoholic beverages if they serve alcohol to minors (people below the legal drinking age).

You should also be aware that there are very strict laws against drinking just before or while driving a car. In some places it is illegal to have an open can or bottle of alcohol in a car.

In some places there are laws that control the place or time when alcohol can be drunk or served. For example, in some places alcohol cannot be sold on Sunday. In some public places (beaches, parks), you cannot drink alcohol. Be careful.

Smoking is now prohibited in most public places. Look for signs. If you are not sure, ask somebody. Smoking also is not acceptable in many private homes. In most places, you must be 18 to purchase cigarettes.

1.5 Hotels

Motels, inns, and **hotels** throughout the United States, are similar. The main difference between them is the type of building and location. Motels were originally built along highways to serve long-distance travelers. They are often only one or two stories high and are long narrow buildings where you can park your car in front of the room you are staying in. They are often found outside of the center of town. Hotels and inns are often larger, more formal and expensive, and offer more services.

Hotels and motels are not required to post rates, so it is a good idea to ask when you check in (arrive and register). In a typical room you will find:

- two single or double beds or a king sized bed (you can usually request what you want)

- a telephone and telephone directory

- a private bathroom with towels and soap

- a television

- individually controlled heating and air conditioning

- a closet for your clothes and luggage

- writing supplies (paper, envelopes, and postcards)

- electrical outlets

- drinkable tap water, glasses, and usually a container for ice (an ice bucket); the ice can be obtained from machines located in various places throughout the building.

In addition, many hotels provide a directory of the services provided, such as room service (you telephone an order for food to be delivered to your room) and overnight laundry service. Many places now have Wi-Fi for computer users; you may need to ask for a password. Most hotels have smoking and non-smoking rooms or floors. You should not smoke in a non-smoking area. You may be fined for doing so.

Breakfast and Room Service. Breakfast usually is not included in the room rate. Most hotels and motels have their own restaurant and/or coffee shop where you can obtain meals, but you have to pay in addition to the cost of your room. This is also true of room service. In both cases, you may charge everything to your room number and pay for it when you leave. Room service is more expensive than eating in the hotel coffee shop or restaurant.

Additional Expenses. You should also be aware of two additional hotel/motel expenses. The cost for using the telephone in your room is often very high. It is usually much cheaper to use a phone card or your own cell phone. Motels do not have people to help you with your luggage, but hotels do. They are called "bell-hops," and they expect a tip. One dollar ($1) for each bag is acceptable.

Hostels and Ys. Less expensive places to stay are youth hostels and YMCAs/YWCAs (Young Men's/Women's Christian Association). You do not need to be a "youth" or a "Christian" to stay in a youth hostel or a YMCA/YWCA; all you need is a pass, which you can obtain in your own country or at a hostel in the United States. Hostels provide simple dormitory sleeping arrangements with a community kitchen. You can obtain information at hiusa.org/usa-hostels, hostelworld.com, or in the *Hostel Guide and Handbook* published annually by American Youth Hostels. Write to 20 West 17th Street, New York, NY 10011. Most YWCAs and YMCAs have overnight accommodations, and they are usually centrally located in large cities. Their rates are about half those of hotels, and both members and non-members are welcome. They are referred to informally as "*the* Y," and usually have a swimming pool, gymnasium facilities, and sometimes cultural and social events.

Bob and Bobbie's

B&B

Your home away from home.
Welcome!

Bed and Breakfast Another kind of hotel, called a bed and breakfast or B and B, is similar to the European *pension*. The building is actually a large private home that has been converted to a small inn for overnight visitors. The price of the room includes a good breakfast. Staying in a bed and breakfast will bring you in close contact with local people. Tourist offices or the local Chamber of Commerce in most towns will have listings of B and B's.

1.6 Telephone

Yellow Pages. In addition to the Internet, one of your best guidebooks will be the Yellow Pages in the telephone directory ("telephone book"). You will find almost every kind of service listed in the Yellow Pages – for example, restaurants, hotels, travel agents, banks, schools, medical centers, automobile repair, etc., etc. There are phone books in most hotel rooms.

Cell phones have become popular in the United States as they have around the world. More than 75% of Americans have them, and the old landlines (home phones and coin operated pay phones) are disappearing. You may want to get a cell phone for convenience if you will be staying in America and traveling. Calls will be billed to your account, or you can purchase a cell phone that has pre-paid minutes. When your minutes are used up, you can purchase more minutes. This may be an advantage if you don't want to sign a longterm contract for a cell phone. A popular alternative to cell phones, if you travel with a computer, is Skype.™

Pay phones, public telephones, can still be found at airports and other transportation terminals, and in some gas stations, hotel lobbies, malls, and shopping centers. To use one, you will need coins for most local calls. The phone will not give change, so if you do not have exact change, do not expect to get anything back from what you put in. If you are paying for the call with coins, the operator will check to make sure you have enough change before the call is put through. If you use up the time allowed by your initial deposit, you will asked for more coins.

If you don't want to pay for a call with coins, you can charge it or place your call collect on long-distance calls. If you call collect, the person you are calling will have to pay for the call by "accepting the charges." A phone card is much less expensive.

Phone Cards. For travelers without cell phones, the easiest way to make a long-distance call is to use a phone card. You can buy one at many stores or post offices. Their cost depends on the number of minutes on the card. The directions on the back of the card explain how to use the card. Phone cards can be used on any phone; there is a small extra charge for using a phone card at a pay phone. With some phone cards, extra time can be added for an additional charge.

Credit Card Calls. Recently, a new kind of phone has been installed, usually found in airports where regular, coin-operated phones are also located. These phones are designed to be used only with credit cards. They do not take money, and you cannot use them unless you have a credit card. In some cases, you can pass the magnetic strip on your credit card through a slot on the phone, or you may be able to use the buttons.

"800" Numbers. Many businesses offer an 800 number. This means it does not cost you money to call them. To use this service, first dial 1, then 800, 866, 877, or 888, and then the seven-digit number. Other companies offer services using a 900 number. These services are generally information and entertainment, and the cost is charged to your phone bill. These services are often very expensive.

Area Codes. Telephone numbers are preceded by a three-digit area code number, which generally is different from state to state. Most states have more than one area code number.

Directory Assistance. One useful number is 411. This is for directory assistance – to find a telephone number you don't know. You can use it anywhere in the United States. Sometimes there is a charge. Cell phone numbers are not listed.

911. In an emergency when you need the police, fire department, or an ambulance, you can dial 911 for free from most places in the United States. In some places this will put you in touch immediately with the police. In other places, 911 will reach a special operator. You can, of course, simply dial 0 to reach a regular operator, but that takes a little more time. Saving a few minutes can make the difference between life and death in some emergencies.

Time Zones. There are four time zones in the United States, so there is a three-hour time difference between New York and California. (9:00 a.m. in New York is 6:00 a.m. in California). Check the telephone book or the Internet for the time difference to the place you are calling. See the map on the next page.

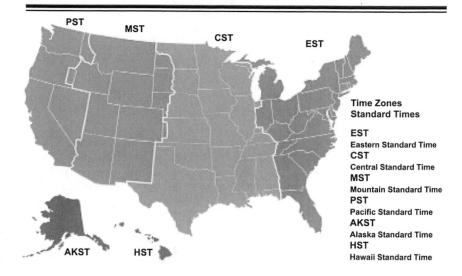

Time Zones
Standard Times

EST
Eastern Standard Time
CST
Central Standard Time
MST
Mountain Standard Time
PST
Pacific Standard Time
AKST
Alaska Standard Time
HST
Hawaii Standard Time

1.7 Mail, Faxes, and Email

Post offices in the United States are usually open from 8:00 a.m. to 5:00 or 6:00 p.m. Monday through Friday, and until noon on Saturday. They are closed on national holidays. You can purchase stamps at any post office, as well as at hotel desks and from coin-operated vending machines located in transportation terminals. Postal rates are based on weight and destination and are changed from time to time, so you should check the cost of mailing letters and postcards when you arrive.

Letters can be mailed at a post office or in red, white, and blue mailboxes located on many street corners in American cities. There is a sign on each mailbox which states the time when the mail will be taken from the box, so you can check to see when your mail is actually going out.

If you want to receive mail while traveling, it can be sent to you c/o General Delivery, Main Post Office, in the town where you expect to be. All general delivery mail must be picked up by you in person, and you will be asked to show identification.

The usual form for a mailing address is:
Name
House or apartment number and street
City, state, ZIP code number

ZIP Code. The ZIP code number is important. If you don't know it, you should ask at a post office. They will give you the number.

Packages can be sent from any U.S. Post Office. The Postal Service (USPS) offers standard "flat-rate" envelopes and boxes called Priority Mail. The Post Office says, "If it fits, it ships," meaning the weight does not matter. There are also special Post Office rates for library mail and printed matter, but it is illegal to include personal letters in these packages.

United Parcel Service (UPS) also handles packages. UPS Ground service is sometimes more expensive than the Post Office, but the packages are insured and trackable. UPS will also pick up packages at your residence for an additional charge.

Express Delivery. There are several express services that offer overnight service for letters and packages; Federal Express, DHL, the Post Office's Express Mail, and UPS are the largest. These carriers also offer a less expensive second-day delivery. They are very reliable and fast. Check the Internet or look in the telephone book for phone numbers and addresses.

Texting, Email, and Fax. Many people who use smart phones prefer texting (sending a typed message) to telephoning. People who have computers now communicate on the internet using email. Texting and emailing are fast, inexpensive ways to send written messages. In fact, they have reduced the mail sent through the Post Office. Social networking (Facebook and Twitter) is also very popular in the U.S. and all around the world. Sending information by fax is common, particularly in business. You can do this from a computer or at a shop that specializes in printing and photocopying.

1.8 Transportation

Air travel. To travel within the United States, there are four basic ways: plane, train, bus, and car. Each way has advantages and disadvantages. Air travel between major cities is, of course, the fastest way. Domestic air travel is generally expensive. However, less expensive fares are often available on special "shuttle" flights and as promotions. Travel agents can suggest the least expensive flights. Many people make their reservations "on-line," through the Internet.

Amtrak. The national passenger railway system is called Amtrak. For seeing the countryside in comfort, this is the best way to travel. However, trains are expensive for longer trips. Sometimes special rates are available for tourists. Buses are cheaper than planes and trains, and buses go to many more places. Riding for a long distance in a bus, however, is not so comfortable.

Driving. Using a **car** is definitely the easiest way to travel because you can leave, stop, and go when you want. It can also be the cheapest if you share your expenses with other people. The highway system in the United States is very well developed. The Interstate Highway System allows you to travel across the entire country without stopping for traffic lights. There are rest areas and restaurant/gas station areas all along the Interstates. The speed limit on the Interstates varies from state to state; it is always posted on signs. Within each state, the maximum speed limit may be 65 or 75 miles per hour, but in special zones it will be lower. On other roads, it is usually lower. Some highways are toll roads, which means you must pay to use the road with cash or an electronic pass on your windshield – these have various names, EZ Pass, FastTrack, etc.

Car Rental. If you do not have your own car, you can rent one. There are many car rental agencies, and some are cheaper than others. Use the Internet or call on the telephone and ask for rates, which can be per day or per mile or both. You pay for gas. You must have a credit card and, of course, a driver's license with your photo. If you are a tourist, you may use your own national driver's license. In cities you can become a member of Zipcar or similar companies. Your card allows you to use a car whenever you need one. Check the Internet to see how it works.

Traffic Laws. In smaller cities and towns, Americans usually are careful to obey traffic signs and regulations. They often stop or slow down to let other cars in and out of the traffic pattern. Be very careful at pedestrian crossings. If you see a person trying to cross at a crosswalk, you must stop.

Parking. In most cities you can get around on foot, or by bus, taxi, car, or subway (in large cities). Because of the heavy traffic and limited parking, a car is not always useful in a large city. If you do bring your car to a city, you can park on the street at designated places. These parking spaces usually have parking meters, which require coins. Read the instructions carefully, and do not let the meter expire. The police check carefully and, if the meter shows a little red "expired" flag, you will get a parking ticket, which can be very expensive – $50.00 or more in some large cities. A better place to park is a parking garage. It is more expensive, but it is safer and you don't need to come back to put more money in the meter. Wherever you park in a large city, lock the car and keep packages out of sight. Car stealing is a big problem in cities.

Buses and Taxis. Every city and town has its own public transportation system, and each system is a little different. One thing you should know is that buses often require exact change. (You can ask someone who is waiting at a bus stop.) Taxi (cab) drivers also carry very little change, so have small bills with you when you "take a cab." The taxi drivers expect a tip (see section 1.12). Some taxis accept credit cards. If you want to use one, ask before you get in.

Bicycles. In smaller towns and rural areas, public transportation is not very good. Most people depend on cars. In warm weather, bicycles are popular. In many cities it is possible to rent a bicycle from an automated bicycle rack.

Hitchhiking. You may think about hitchhiking, standing by the roadside holding out your arm and pointing down the road with your thumb. It is the least expensive and most dangerous way to travel. We do not advise you to do this.

1.9 Shopping

Most **businesses and offices** in the United States are open from 9:00 a.m. to 5:00 p.m. Monday through Friday, except on holidays. Employees take an hour-long lunch break sometime between noon and 2:00 p.m., but they take breaks at different times so there is always someone to help customers.

Retail stores operate on a slightly different schedule. Most stores in the city center open at 9:00 or 10:00 a.m. and close at 5:30 or 6:00 p.m., except on Fridays, when they often stay open later. They are open on Saturday and during lunch hours. Larger stores are often open longer hours and on Sundays and holidays.

Malls and **Shopping Centers.** Outside the city centers you will find these shopping areas. You usually need a car to get there, but parking is free. In shopping centers several stores share a parking lot. Malls are shopping areas with many different stores and restaurants all under one roof. They are heated and air-conditioned and generally safe. They also stay open until 9:00 p.m., and they are usually open on Sunday.

Supermarkets sell food, and they are usually open from 6:00 a.m. until late in the evening. In most towns and cities there will be at least one that is open all day and night, seven days a week.

Coops. Local supermarkets that are owned by their customers are called coops. They generally specialize in health food and locally grown produce but also carry a wide range of other food and household items.

Specialty Shops. These are small stores which carry only one or two kinds of merchandise, such as shoes, clothing, books, stationery, antiques, jewelry, hardware, etc.

Chain Stores. These stores operate throughout the country and carry clothing, household goods and appliances, hardware, and furniture at reasonable prices. Some well-known chain stores are JC Penney and Sears. There are also discount chain stores. Some well-known ones are WalMart, Target, Home Depot, and Staples.

Department Stores. These stores are very large and have a wide variety of products. The products are organized into different departments, such as men's, women's, and children's clothing, housewares, furniture, appliances, fabric, toys, etc.

Factory Outlets. These retail stores are run by the manufacturers. They sell their own products at lower prices than those charged by other retail stores. These outlets are often located outside the city center.

Convenience Stores. These small stores are open all day and late into the evening. They sell basic food items, tobacco, newspapers, and other small items. Their prices are usually higher than those at supermarkets, but they are often close to your home and open when you need them.

Gas Stations. Gas, oil, and other supplies for cars are easily available in the suburbs, in small towns, and along highways. There are few gas stations in the centers of big cities. Nowadays, most stations are self-service. This means you have to pump your own gas. In most places, you pay first with a credit card or cash, then pump. In other places, you pump first and pay after. A sign will tell you what to do. Some stations have full-service pumps. This means an attendant will pump your gas. The attendant may also check your oil and clean your window, if you ask. The attendant does not expect to be tipped.

Some gas stations sell tires and do tire repair, but not all. A few stations have a mechanic to do engine repairs. The Internet and Yellow Pages always list local sources for auto care. Inside many gas stations, there is a small convenience store. Most towns have at least one 24-hour gas station.

Auto clubs like **AAA** (American Automobile Association, known as "Triple A") provide maps and travel advice as well as emergency service, towing, and mechanical help to members.

Drug Stores. Over-the-counter or patent medicines are available in many kinds of stores. Stronger or special medicines are available only in drug stores or pharmacies. They must be prescribed by a doctor. In the U.S., pharmacists cannot prescribe medicines; they only prepare them with a doctor's order. Prescription and name-brand medicines are generally expensive, and the pharmacist may sell a generic medicine that does the same thing for less money. Drug stores also sell many other things. They are like small department stores.

Sales Tax. There in no general federal sales tax, although the federal government does tax gasoline and diesal fuels for vehicles. Most states (and some cities) have a sales tax of 2% to 10%. Most states do not tax food for consumption at home. A few do not tax clothing. In many states there is also a room and meals tax on hotel and restaurant bills.

1.10 Health, Medical Care, and Safety

Health Insurance. The United States is changing its medical care and insurance system, but everyone will still need to have insurance. Without it, medical care is very expensive. You should purchase health insurance to cover medical expenses in case you have an accident or get sick. This is very important. For information, ask about health insurance at the U.S. embassy or consulate when you get your visa.

Hospitals. If you need medical care while traveling, you can call any hospital. Some hospitals have outpatient clinics, or they may help you in the emergency room, but this is *very* expensive. To save you money, the hospital also may give you the name and telephone number of a doctor or a clinic in the neighborhood. There are not many government-supported hospitals in the United States. Most hospitals are private, nonprofit organizations, and their fees are very high.

Water is safe to drink in all American towns and cities.

Personal Safety. It is unfortunate but necessary to say that visitors need to be careful about their personal safety, especially in large cities. If you are not familiar with a place, do not explore it alone, especially at night and on foot. First, ask somebody (hosts, hotel personnel, police) for advice on where to go and where NOT to go. While driving, keep car doors locked and windows closed, and do not get out of the car or open the window if you are stopped by someone other than the police. Do not open hotel room doors unless you know who is outside. Do not show cash openly.

1.11 Electricity and Electronics

The electric current in the United States is 110–115 volts, 60-cycle AC rather than the 200–220 volts, 50-cycle AC found in many other countries. Larger machines such as clothes dryers require special 200–220–volt outlets. Smaller appliances such as shavers, hair dryers, and curlers will work on the lower current. For other appliances, you may need a transformer to change the current to a higher voltage. All plugs in the United States are flat-pronged rather than round. You can purchase adapters to attach to round plugs so they can be used in a flat-pronged outlet.

1.12 Tipping

How Much and Who? In restaurants, the usual tip for waiters is 15%-20% (see section 1.3). In most fast food restaurants, you do not tip. In hotels and motels, you leave a tip for the maid only if you stay several days. You should tip 10%–15% for hotel room service people and $1.00 per bag for bellhops. Barbers and hairdressers are usually tipped about 10%–15%, and taxi drivers also expect 10%–15%.

Service Included? Before tipping room service people and waiters, look at your bill to be sure that a service charge has not been included. For many services when you pay by credit card, you will find a place to add a tip to the credit card slip. Some people prefer to pay tips in cash so the specific person they are tipping gets the money.

Don't Tip. The following people are not usually tipped in the United States: theater ushers, hotel desk clerks, guides at historical sites, mail carriers, grocery store employees, gas station attendants, and elevator operators.

1.13 Measures

The United States has not adopted the metric system. The following charts will help you to understand and convert to U.S. measurements.

Linear Measurements

U.S.	Metric
1 inch	2.54 centimeters
1 foot	0.3048 meter
1 yard	0.9144 meter
1 mile	1.609 kilometers

Metric	U.S.
1 centimeter	0.39 inch
1 meter	3.28 feet / 1.094 yards
1 kilometer	0.62 mile

Liquid Measurements

U.S.	Metric
1 teaspoon (tsp)	5 milliliters
1 tablespoon (tbsp)	15 milliliters
1 cup (c)	0.237 liter
1 pint (pt)	0.473 liter
1 quart (qt)	0.946 liter
1 gallon (gal)	3.785 liters

Metric	U.S.
1 liter	2.1 pints / 1.05 quarts

Dry Measurements

U.S.	Metric
1 pint	0.551 liter
1 quart	1.1 liters
1 peck	8.81 liters
1 bushel	35.24 liters

Weights

U.S.	Metric
1 ounce	28.4 grams
1 pound	454 grams
1 ton	0.907 ton

Metric	U.S.
1 gram	0.035 ounce
1 kilogram (kilo)	2.2 pounds
1 ton	1.1 tons

Formulas for Approximate Conversions

1. Yards to meters, multiply by 0.9.
   Meters to yards, multiply by 1.1.

2. Miles to kilometers, multiply by 1.6.
   Kilometers to miles, multiply by 0.6.

3. 1 quart is about 1 liter.
   1 gallon is about 4 liters.

4. 1 pound is about 0.45 kilos.
   1 kilo is about 2.2 pounds.

Temperature

Fahrenheit	Celsius
100°F	37.8°C
90°F	32.2°C
80°F	26.7°C
70°F	21.1°C
60°F	15.6°C
50°F	10.0°C
40°F	4.4°C
32°F	0°C
10°F	–12°C
0°F	–17.8°C
–10°F	–23°C

Celsius	Fahrenheit
100°C	212°F
40°C	104°F
30°C	86°F
20°C	68°F
10°C	50°F
0°C	32°F
–10°C	14°F
–20°C	–4°F

The Fahrenheit temperature is approximately twice the Celsius plus 30:

$$C° \times 2 + 30 = \text{approx. } F°$$

$$(F° - 30)/2 = \text{approx. } C°$$

Clothing Sizes

Women *Skirts, dresses, coats*		Men *Coats, jackets*	
U.S.	**Europe**	**U.S.**	**Europe**
10	38	36	46
12	40	38	48
14	42	40	50
16	44	42	54
18	46	44	56
20	48	46	59
Blouses, sweaters		*Shirts*	
30	38	14	36
32	40	$14^1/_2$	37
34	42	15	38
36	44	$15^1/_2$	39
38	46	16	40
40	48	$16^1/_2$	41
		17	42
Shoes		*Shoes*	
5	35	8	41
$5^1/_2$	35	$8^1/_2$	42
6	36	$9 - 9^1/_2$	43
7	38	$10 - 10^1/_2$	44
8	$38^1/_2$	$11 - 11^1/_2$	45
$8^1/_2$	39	$12 - 12^1/_2$	46
9	40	13	47

2. Customs and Values

The topics in this section will help you understand American culture — the way Americans think and believe and act. We will make generalizations that may not be true for the people you meet, live, or study with. One generalization which you should always remember is that there is great variety among the states of America and the people of America. It is a culture formed from many cultures.

2.1 Greetings and Leave-takings

Greetings. Americans do not use long greetings. They say, *"Hello"* or *"Hi, how are you?"* or *"Howdy"* or *"How are you doing?"*

People usually shake hands when they meet for the first time. However, young people may not do this. Sometimes, Americans neglect to introduce new people to one another. This is not a problem. Most people are comfortable introducing themselves if nobody introduces them. You should give your name when someone introduces themself to you. If you don't, they will then ask your name. When someone older is introduced, they will usually say *"How do you do?"* or *"Nice to meet you."* Young people may just say *"Hi."*

Leave-takings are also often brief. *"'Bye"* or *"See you later"* usually is enough. It is also common, when people say goodbye, for them to say *"It's been nice to meet you,"* and they may add, *"We should get together sometime,"* or *"You should come over sometime,"* or *"I'll call you soon."* Don't be disappointed if someone says, *"I'll call you,"* and never does, or suggests that you come over sometime and never invites you. These are all formulas; they do not necessarily mean that the person will actually do what they have suggested.

2.2 Names and Titles

Titles based on social class are not used in the United States. Some titles based on occupation, such as **Ambassador, Senator, Governor, Father, Rabbi,** and **Imam**, are used. Other occupations that usually carry titles are: court judge, military officer, and medical or academic doctor. Individuals in other occupations are usually referred to with **Mr.** ("mister") and **Ms** (pronounced "mizz") followed by the last or family name. You will hear the older titles **Miss** for unmarried women and **Mrs.** ("missiz") for married women, but most professional women usually prefer Ms. Listen. If someone is introduced as Reverend, Professor, or Miss, use that title.

Many people do not like to use titles and last names. If a person is introduced to you as "Doctor Johnson," do not be surprised if they say "Call me Bob." In this case, you will be too formal if you continue to say "Doctor Johnson."

As a general rule, young people should address older people as Mr., Ms, Miss, or Mrs., or a title. This is polite. It is quite normal to say, *"Hello, Mrs. Brown"* but not *"Hello, Mrs."* Using occupation titles alone is generally OK – *"Hello, Doctor."*

2.3 Conversation Topics

Questions. Americans often ask a lot of questions when they first meet someone, and some of these questions may seem quite personal to you. When an American does this, they are only looking for a common ground for building a relationship. Perhaps you will discover similar interests or abilities which can then be used as a basis for friendship.

Topics to Avoid. Although Americans ask a lot of questions, until you know a person well, there are some topics that you should avoid in conversation: the person's age and financial status, the cost of the person's clothes or personal belongings, their personal religious beliefs, and their love (or sex) life.

2.4 Friendship

Americans are open and friendly to newcomers. Perhaps this is because they are very mobile, and they have learned to make new friends quickly. This easy friendliness does not mean, however, that they will try to develop a long and deep friendship with you. This kind of relationship takes time in the United States, as it does anywhere. Remember, people often move from one town to another, so it is not easy for them to develop long-lasting friendships.

2.5 Invitations

Guest Status. Americans will quickly and easily invite strangers into their homes. You will find that you are treated as "one of the family" almost immediately after you arrive. Do not be surprised at American informality. It is quite common. Your hosts will probably not give you very special guest status. You should "make yourself at home" with them. If you are invited to a home for a meal or a party, you can ask, *"Can I bring anything?"* If you are invited for a stay of one night or more, then it is appropriate to bring a small gift – flowers, candy, or some souvenir from your own country.

Written Invitation. If you receive a written invitation, it is important to respond to it as soon as possible. Some invitations will have **R.S.V.P.** or "Please reply" written at the bottom, and these must have a reply. If a telephone number is given, then it is polite to call and accept or decline the invitation. If there is no phone number, then a written note is adequate. If you receive an invitation over the telephone, make sure that you have correctly understood the date, time, and location. And if for some reason you should realize later that you cannot attend, then be sure to telephone to tell the person inviting you that you will not be there, and explain the reason why.

2.6 Personal Space and Privacy

Touching. These notes on personal space are very general. Customs vary in different parts of the country and with ethnic groups. However, in general, Americans don't touch each other very much in public. Touching between two people of the same sex is not common. (Touching between two men is sometimes considered a sign of homosexuality.) Touching between people of different sex is more common, especially if they are young lovers. You may see young men and women holding hands, embracing, and even kissing in public. In the past, this kind of open touching was considered very impolite. But times are changing, and nowadays people are more likely to touch and show affection in public. In fact, it isn't unusual to hug someone if you have not seen them in a long time, or if they or you are going away.

Gestures. In conversations, Americans stand about 2 to 3 feet apart and often use a lot of gestures. Some gestures involve physical contact. Sympathy is shown by putting a hand on another person's shoulder. Touching the other person's hand or arm shows support, agreement, or thanks.

Privacy. Americans are not especially private people. They leave the doors to their offices open, and often neighboring homes are not separated by fences or walls. It is also rare to find closed doors in homes. The doors to bathrooms are generally left open except when the room is in use. Nevertheless, people are concerned about their privacy when they deal with business and the government, particularly online. They do not want personal information shared by these agencies.

2.7 "On Time"

Being "on time" is important in the United States. A few guidelines are given here.

For a Dinner Invitation. When you are invited for a meal, you should arrive within 5 to 15 minutes of the time specified in the invitation. Do not arrive earlier, because people usually do their own cooking, and they may be working until the last minute to get things ready for you. If you are going to be late, it is polite to call and inform the people who have invited you. Then they can prepare the meal according to the time you will actually arrive.

At Parties. When you are invited to a party, you can arrive up to half an hour "late." For cocktail parties and receptions, a time period is usually specified during which you are expected to arrive and leave. You may arrive at any time during that period, but remember that you are also expected to leave by the ending time indicated.

At Public Events. For movies and theater productions, you will want to arrive at least 10 minutes ahead of time to get your ticket/program and be seated. You should also be at least 10 minutes early for weddings, funerals, lectures, and sports events.

For business appointments, you should arrive exactly on time or a few minutes before your appointment. If the person you are seeing is busy, they may keep you waiting, but you should still be on time.

2.8 Silence

Many Americans are uncomfortable with silence when they are with another person. When there is silence in a conversation, they may start talking to stop the silence. Students often study with music playing in the background, and people working around the house will often have the television or radio on "to keep them company."

If you are silent in a conversation or a gathering for a long time, Americans will try to "draw you out" (get you to talk) and may even ask if you are all right or if there is anything they can do to help you. One important note: Americans may remain silent when you say something they don't agree with because they feel uncomfortable disagreeing with someone they don't know well.

2.9 Equality

Equality. The concept of equality is extremely important in the United States. Americans generally say that all people are born with equal rights, regardless of social, economic, racial, ethnic, or gender differences. They expect to have an equal opportunity to achieve personal and professional goals. Americans can become very angry if they think they are not being given an equal opportunity to compete or improve their lives. Fair government and equal protection by law are very important. Americans may also become angry at people who expect special favors or treatment. When they think someone is not being fair or is looking for special treatment, they are likely to say, "Who do you think you are?" They also get angry at people who will not wait for their turn.

Social and class differences exist in the United States, of course, and there are many inequalities in everyday life. Most people are aware of these inequalities, but they would rather think that the United States is a country where, to quote the Declaration of Independence, "all men are created equal" and have certain rights, and "among these are Life, Liberty and the pursuit of Happiness."

2.10 Independence

Independence and self-reliance are important personal values for Americans. This means that people believe they are responsible for their own happiness and future, and that they should not depend on others to make them happy and successful. This does not mean that they do not work together or help one another or cooperate. It means that each person is responsible for their own life.

Individualism is seen in many aspects of American life. For example, the great American hero, the mythical cowboy, is a strong, independent individual. The emphasis on individualism begins early. Children are encouraged to develop and express their own opinions and interests, particularly in school. In family life, children are often given household responsibilities at an early age. Teenagers are expected to find summer jobs when they are not in school. And American young people often leave home early to live "on their own."

2.11 Eating Customs

Knife and Fork. Americans eat with the fork in the right hand, or if they are left handed, in the left hand. The other hand is usually in the lap. When cutting, they hold the knife in the right hand and the fork in the left. After cutting, the knife is placed on the edge of the plate and the fork is shifted to the right hand for eating.

Here are some other cultural rules that are followed by most Americans when eating.

- Keep your mouth closed when you are chewing food, and speak only when your mouth is empty.
- When you need something that is not near you on the table, ask the person closest to the item to pass it to you; do not reach across in front of them to get it yourself.
- If someone offers you more to eat and you would like to have more, accept their offer. They will not repeat the offer or insist that you eat. If you don't want more, they will accept your refusal.
- Try not to burp after eating.
- Do not rest your arms on the table while you are eating.
- If you need to leave the table while others are still eating, ask, "Would you excuse me, please?"

Breakfast. Most people eat three times a day, and may also have a snack and coffee mid-morning and mid-afternoon. A complete breakfast consists of fruit juice and cereal or eggs. Eggs are usually accompanied by toast and bacon or sausage. Adults drink coffee or tea and children drink milk. Special breakfast dishes served less frequently (typically on weekends and holidays) include waffles, French toast, and pancakes, served with butter and maple syrup.

Lunch is usually eaten during an hour between noon and 2:00 p.m. People at work and school rarely go home for lunch; they bring a lunch with them in a paper bag or lunch box, or buy something. A typical lunch might consist of one or two sandwiches (see section 1.2), a piece of fruit, and sometimes a small bag of chips (potato or corn chips are popular) and/or a few cookies. Many people working in offices will eat at nearby restaurants.

Dinner is the main meal in the United States. It is eaten in the evening, usually after 6:00 p.m. It usually consists of a meat, fish, or poultry dish with cooked vegetables and a starch such as rice or potatoes. Dessert is common in many homes.

Snacks. In some families a late evening snack may be common. Salty or sweet snacks may be eaten while watching television or just before going to bed. Some Americans snack many times during the day, which causes people of all ages to get overweight.

2.12 Family Life

It is difficult to generalize about family life in America. There is a great variety of economic, cultural, and regional lifestyles. However, a few observations can be made.

Typically, **the family unit** that lives together consists of parents and children. Older people do not generally live with their children who have families of their own. They do, however, keep in touch with their children and remain interested in the well-being of their grandchildren. Typical families have one or two parents and one to three children. Today the parents may not be married, and they may be of the same sex. The single-parent family is now much more common than it was in the past because of divorce and unwed pregnancy.

Pets. You will find that Americans often have a family pet – usually a dog or cat. The pet is like one of the family and lives in the house with the people. Americans often talk to their pets and spend a lot of money on them.

Children today often live at home while they are in school or until they get a job. Some may finish college and return to their parents' home to save money. However, traditionally young people are expected to leave their parents' home when they become adults. Career and job opportunities, and marriage, often take young adults far away from their parents. However, the family keeps in touch by phone/texting, email, or mail, and will travel to help one another in times of difficulty or to share holiday celebrations. Americans expect their children to choose their own careers and their own spouses. This is again part of the individualism Americans value so highly (see section 2.10).

Female and Male Roles. Within the society as well as within the family, differences between female and male roles are decreasing. In the past, women had fewer opportunities than men to pursue personal and professional interests because they stayed at home to care for their children. This has changed, and many women are working outside the home. In many families, the man is assuming more responsibility for child rearing and housework in order to allow the woman to develop a professional career. Childen often go to daycare and preschool programs.

Housework. Still, in general, men do not do very much housework. Children, on the other hand, are often given tasks to do on a regular basis, such as setting the table for dinner, watering the garden, folding the laundry, etc. For this work they are often given a sum of money as a weekly allowance. This allowance gives them some responsibility for paying for their personal expenses, such as snacks and tickets to the movies.

The Elderly. Older people usually do not live with their children. Typically, when they retire they prefer to live on their own as long as they are able to take care of themselves. Many travel, visting family and friends or seeing new places. Then they may live in special homes for the aged where their children and grandchildren can come to visit them. Some of the elderly are poor and lonely, and are not given the same degree of respect they receive in many other countries. However, the status of older people is changing. People are living longer and are healthier because of improved medical care. They are becoming politically organized and working to ensure that they will be respected and valued. Many communities provide senior citizen centers where older people can meet and socialize. To attract their business, many stores and businesses give discounts to senior citizens.

2.13 Leisure

Sports of all types are popular in the United States, and facilities for playing various sports exist in all cities and towns: swimming pools, tennis courts, football and baseball fields, golf courses, bowling alleys, skating rinks, skateboard parks, etc. In addition, many Americans have taken up jogging and bicycling in order to stay physically fit. You will probably see joggers almost anywhere you go.

Other popular sports are skateboarding, snowboarding, skiing (on water in warm weather and on snow in the winter), sailing, fishing, hiking, and camping. There are also exercise groups and fitness clubs in most communities. These are groups that do physical exercises to music and centers where exercise equipment is available.

Pastimes. Most American families have at least one television and watch it regularly. Many people listen to the radio. On weekends, going to the movies is a popular pastime, as is going out for a meal at a restaurant. In warm weather, Americans enjoy going to the beach or parks, or they stay at home in their yards to have picnics and barbecues (where food is cooked and eaten outside) and people play outdoor games.

Home Computers. Most homes now have computers, tablets, and smartphones. They are popular modes of communication, using email and Skype.™ Using social networking such as Facebook and Twitter is also common. And computers are used for exploring (surfing) the Internet for information and on-line shopping, and for enjoying music, videos, and reading. Video games are very popular. Many people spend a lot of time playing games on their computers.

Other Activities. Americans like to read, do various crafts, watch sports events, and attend concerts. They also enjoy cooking, gardening, and such "do-it-yourself" projects as sewing their own clothes or building furniture, as might be expected where independence is valued.

2.14 Holidays

The National Holidays: There are ten national holidays. On a national holiday, schools, banks, government offices, and many businesses are closed. The exact date for five of the holidays changes from year to year because these holidays are celebrated on Mondays so people can have a long weekend. Here is a list of national holidays.

New Year's Day — January 1
Martin Luther King, Jr.'s Birthday — 3rd Monday in January
Presidents' Day — 3rd Monday in February
Memorial Day — Last Monday in May
Independence Day — July 4
Labor Day — 1st Monday in September
Columbus Day — 2nd Monday in October
Veterans' Day — November 11
Thanksgiving — 4th Thursday in November
Christmas — December 25

Special holiday celebrations and traditions:

Valentine's Day. On February 14, people give cards, flowers, and candy to each other to celebrate love.

Easter. Celebrated in March or April, Easter Sunday is a religious holiday commemorating Jesus Christ's rise from the dead. Many of its traditions, however, are pagan in origin and are observed in American families even when the religious significance is not. On the night before Easter, an imaginary creature known as the Easter Bunny comes to visit children and leaves a basket filled with candy in the shape of eggs, rabbits (bunnies), and baby chicks. Another tradition is dyeing hard-boiled eggs different colors and painting designs on them. It is common to hide these eggs, as well as candy eggs, for children to look for on Easter Sunday. This is called an Easter egg hunt.

Independence Day. July 4, 1776, was when the thirteen American colonies declared independence from England. "The Fourth" is usually celebrated by parades and picnics with friends and family. There are fireworks displays in the evening.

Thanksgiving. The first Thanksgiving was celebrated by the early Pilgrim settlers in Massachusetts in 1621. It was a celebration of thanks for their first successful harvest. They had experienced difficulty in those early times and survived only with the help of Native Americans who taught them how to grow and harvest foods such as squash and corn. The Pilgrims' Thanksgiving lasted three days and was celebrated with their Native American friends. Today, Thanksgiving is a four-day holiday for most Americans, many of whom travel home for a family celebration. The major meal is served on Thursday and usually includes certain traditional dishes: roast turkey, potatoes and yams, cranberry sauce, vegetables, and pumpkin and/or mincemeat pie for dessert.

Halloween. Halloween is celebrated on October 31st and, like Easter, includes pagan customs although its name has religious origins. The name is a shortened version of All Hallow's Eve, the night before All Saints' Day, which is celebrated by some religious groups on November 1st.

Halloween is customarily celebrated by children who dress up in costumes and go "trick-or-treating." Wearing their costumes, they go to various homes and offer adults an alternative: a "trick" (some mischief they will do to the adult) or a "treat" such as candy (which the adult can give to keep the children from doing mischief). The threat of a trick is not taken seriously today. Halloween is a favorite holiday with children and is often celebrated in school.

Christmas, Hanukkah, and Kwanzaa. These holidays are celebrated in December. All are celebrated with lights during the darkest time of the year.

Christmas is celebrated on December 25th to commemorate the birth of Jesus Christ. There are many customs associated with this holiday: exchanging gifts; Santa Claus, who leaves toys for children under the Christmas tree the night before Christmas; decorating the home with evergreens; singing Christmas carols; and sending Christmas cards to friends and acquaintances. Christmas is officially a national holiday and is celebrated in some way by many non-Christians as well as Christians.

Hanukkah is the Jewish Festival of Lights, a celebration of religious freedom. The actual date depends on the Jewish calendar, but it is always celebrated in December and lasts for eight days.

Kwanzaa, beginning on December 26th, is a seven-day holiday based on an African harvest festival; it celebrates the diversity of cultures and religions in Africa and around the world. As with Hanukkah, traditional wisdom is shared with children while ceremonial candles are lit each day.

New Year's Eve. New Year's Eve is celebrated on December 31st with parties that last beyond midnight so that everyone can celebrate the first minutes of the New Year. In many places the celebrations are called "First Night." New Year's Day, January 1st, is celebrated with parades in some cities.

2.15 The Environment

Pollution. In recent years Americans have become more and more conscious of the natural environment and the problems of pollution. For that reason, waste disposal is important. Do not throw litter (paper, cans, bottles) on the roadside or in parks or even in the forest. Many Americans become very angry when they see someone littering, and in many places there is a heavy fine for littering.

Recycling. In many places it is important to separate and recycle (use again) paper and cardboard, and certain plastic, glass, and aluminum containers. In some places this material is picked up by a waste disposal truck. In other places you must take it to a recycling center.

2.16 Business Etiquette

Cothing. In the business world, it is customary for men to wear a tie with a business suit or, in a less formal office, a tie with a sports jacket and slacks. Women wear a business suit or a dress. A suit with dress pants is less formal. Until you know the office, it is best to be formal.

Time. It is very important to be on time for business meetings and appointments. Always try to arrive at least five minutes before the scheduled time. If you must be late, telephone ahead to say that you will not be on time, and, when you arrive, always apologize and give an explanation for being late. When you first arrive at the office, it is a good idea to ask the receptionist how much time you have. Then you will have an idea about when the meeting will end.

Visiting. The American businessperson will probably greet you with a handshake, a smile, and an offer of coffee or tea. It is not necessary to accept the offer. You should expect that smoking will not be allowed. It is a good idea to offer your business card at this time, especially if your name is a little difficult for an American to say.

Conversation. The first few minutes of the conversation will probably be "small talk" about the weather, your trip, your impressions of America or the city you are in. Let the American host shift the conversation to business. You should look at the person you are talking with, but look away frequently; do not stare, and do not wear sunglasses. It is important to be direct, but it is not good to be very direct or aggressive, nor is it good to be very vague or indecisive. If you have a colleague and you talk to each other in your native language, tell your American host what you are talking about.

Using Names. At first, you should address people as "Mr." or "Ms.," but after a few minutes the American may begin to call you by your first name. This is fairly common, and it is OK for you to do the same.

Ending a Visit. When you think the meeting is coming to an end, you should take a minute to be sure that you understand what the next step will be. When the meeting ends, you will be expected to shake hands again.

Lunch Invitations. In some cases you may be invited to lunch. You will not be expected to pay for the lunch or even to share the bill. If you invite an American to lunch, however, you should pay. They may try to pay or share the bill, and if they are very insistent you can suggest that they pay for the taxi or leave the tip. When an American offers to share the bill, it is not because they think you are poor, but rather because in America, people like to think that the best relationships are those based on an equal footing.

3. Country Facts

As you become more comfortable living in the United States, you may want to know more information about the country — for example, how it is organized and governed. This section includes information about the history, people, and institutions of the United States.

3.1 History

The first inhabitants of North, South, and Central America came about 50,000 years ago from Asia. These aboriginal peoples are called Native American Indians and First Nations. The first Europeans to come were probably the Vikings, who arrived about 1000 A.D. from Greenland but did not establish permanent settlements.

Christopher Columbus is credited with "discovering" America in 1492. This "discovery" caused much excitement in Europe, and explorers from several countries began exploring various parts of the "new" continents during the 1500s. The Spanish and Portuguese explored the Southern Hemisphere. The Spanish conquered the powerful empires of the Incas in Peru and the Aztecs in Mexico. Then they started settlements in what is now the western United States as far north as northern California. Later the British, Dutch, and French explored the east coast of North America, establishing permanent settlements there. The French settlements became eastern Canada; the British and Dutch settlements became the United States.

The Colonies. By the 1700s, there were thirteen British colonies along the east coast of what is now the United States. They stretched from New Hampshire in the north to Georgia in the south. Each colony had a legislature made up of colonists but was under the control of Great Britain.

Economic opportunity and religious and political freedom attracted increasing numbers of settlers to the British colonies. Most came from Britain, but people from almost every other western European country also came. The colonists rejected the idea that government was something inherited from the past. They regarded it as something they themselves should design and control, and although they lived under British rule, they often did not follow British laws.

Relations with Britain became worse during the 1700s. The British tried to tighten control over the colonies by passing laws that restricted freedoms and increased taxes, but the Americans had been governing themselves and had developed their own sense of self-government. Controls from Britain were resented, and this resentment eventually developed into conflict in 1775, when the **Revolutionary War** began. In 1783 the British were finally defeated and forced to accept American independence.

Independence. On July 4, 1776, the colonists declared independence from England with the **Declaration of Independence**. The writers of the declaration set forth certain "truths" that they felt were self-evident: that all men are created equal and are endowed by their Creator with rights to life, liberty, and the pursuit of happiness, and that governments were formed to protect those rights and should therefore derive their powers from the consent of the people they govern. In 1781 a new government was set up under laws called the **Articles of Confederation**. These were not successful, and in 1788 they were replaced by the **U.S. Constitution**. This outlined the basic form of government for the nation and is still the basis for American government and laws today (see section 3.4).

Slavery and Civil War. The main political and social issue causing disagreement among the American states in the 1800s was **slavery**. Slaves were the main work force for the plantation system of farming used in the South. Slavery was first outlawed in the northern states, but the southern states continued the tradition because it provided cheap labor. The southern states tried to secede from the Union but were told by the North that the United States must be preserved. So in 1861 the **Civil War** broke out between the North and the South. This was the most tragic period of United States history; thousands of lives were lost and large parts of the South were left in ruins. The North won the war in 1865, and slavery was outlawed throughout the country soon thereafter.

Settling the West. Throughout the 1800s, settlers moved farther and farther west, and by 1890 settlements had been established all across the country to the Pacific coast. The settlement of the West brought disaster to many of **the Native American tribes.** The Natives had no chance against the superior numbers and weapons of the settlers, and those who fought back were killed or forced to live in certain areas called reservations. By 1900 the Native American way of life had almost become a thing of the past.

Driven from land given to his people by a U.S. treaty, Chief Joseph of the Nez Perce tried to escape to Canada in the winter of 1877. He was tracked down and surrendered in Montana. He said, *"It is cold, and we have no blankets; the little children are freezing to death. My people, some of them, have run away to the hills, and have no blankets, no food. No one knows where they are—perhaps freezing to death. I want to have time to look for my children, and see how many of them I can find. Maybe I shall find them among the dead. Hear me, my chiefs! I am tired; my heart is sick and sad. From where the sun now stands, I will fight no more forever."*

1870-1918. After the Civil War, from 1870 to 1916, the American economy again grew rapidly, driven by increasing agricultural production (as new farms spread across the Great Plains) and rapid industrial growth (stimulated by the expansion of the railroad system, technological inventions, and immigration). The value of goods produced during this period increased ten times, and the country grew in many ways as a result. In 1917, the United States entered into **World War I** in Europe and played an important role until the war ended on November 11, 1918. This cost many lives but also stimulated the economy. After the war the economic growth continued. The weathy invested in all kinds of industries and businesses. Speculators invested in the stock market, which went up and up. People of all kinds borrowed money, betting that the boom would continue.

The Great Depression. Then in 1929 the stock market collapsed and banks began to fail. The Great Depression began. Within a few years, millions of workers lost their jobs. In 1932 the new President, Franklin Roosevelt, said, *"We have nothing to fear but fear itself."* He was right, but the people had lost confidence; they were frightened. The American Dream was a nightmare. There were many reasons for the collapse. Bad industrial and labor practices in the U.S., revolutions and political instability in Europe, China, India, and Mexico disrupting world trade, and a ten-year drought in the Great Plains starting in 1930. The drought and ignorant farming practices caused an environmental disaster called the The Great Dust Bowl. People starved.

Many other countries had similar problems, and as a result, ruthless nationalist leaders gained power in Germany, Italy, and Japan with promises of changing the economic situation. Adolf Hitler in Germany and a group of military leaders in Japan began conquering neighboring countries. In the Soviet Union (Russia), Stalin, the communist dictator, purged all opposition and built up his secret police and his military.

World War II. Their actions led to World War II. From 1941 to 1945, the United States along with its allies fought and won the war. First, Nazi Germany was defeated, caught between the Soviet Union (U.S.S.R.) on the east and on the west the U.S. and Great Britain, with help from the free French, Canadians, and several other allies. The Allies including Australia, and China then turned to defeat the Japanese by pushing them off the mainland of Asia and off one Pacific island after another, moving closer to the home islands of Japan itself. Rather than invade Japan, causing a terrible loss of life among both the Allied troops and the Japanese, President Harry Truman made the decision to try the new, secret weapon the United States had been developing, the atomic bomb. After a second bomb was dropped, the Japanese surrendered.

The Marshall Plan. Following World War II, under the leadership of President Truman and General George Marshall, who had been the head of the allied war effort and who was now Secretary of State, the United States tried a new experiment. For the first time in history, the winner of a war rebuilt the nations it had defeated. New democratic governments were started by the Germans and the Japanese, governments that accepted many of the ideals and the civil rights of the American system. Then under the Marshall Plan, the American government rebuilt the economies of the defeated nations. This brought on a long period of general peace and prosperity.

Economic Growth. Beginning with the end of the war, the United States began its greatest period of economic growth. Roads were built, opening the whole country to truck and automobile traffic. This stimulated the automotive and petroleum industries. Many other new businesses grew quickly, driven by the expanding consumer economy and trade within the United States and internationally.

The American Dream. The Depression wasn't forgotten, but victory in war and the healthy economy restored most Americans' faith in "the American Dream." This is the idea that in America you are free to work hard and save and invest your money so you can live a good life and maybe get rich; if you are educated and smart and work very hard, you may get very rich, and you have a right to do so. Behind the Dream is faith in "the free enterprise system," including the old idea that the rich have a right to power and privilege. In the post-war world, this was explained more positively: uncontrolled competition is good; it stimulates creativity, hard work, and prosperity for everyone, not just the rich. The prosperous began to believe that free enterprise is basic to American democracy, that it is the same as "the pursuit of happiness," one of the basic human rights promised in the Declaration of Independence.

Problems. However, the United States is never simple. Peace brought prosperity, but as the country became richer and more powerful, there were new problems. Progressives saw that many people were still poor and hungry. They felt that in a rich country this was unjust.

The Cold War. Internationally, the Soviet Union had also won WWII, but it had suffered terribly. To strengthen his country, Stalin, its leader, was determined to take over as much of the world as possible for Communism. As the war ended, the U.S. and its new allies, NATO (North Atlantic Treaty Organization) and Japan, began the long competition with the Soviet Union and other communist countries called the Cold War. Winston Churchill, the British Prime Minister, said that an "Iron Curtain" came down across Europe, and he spoke of the "balance of terror," the fear of the atom and hydrogen bombs, that the Americans and Russians developed, kept the major powers from starting WWIII. The Cold War became an "arms race" and a long series of regional wars.

The Arms Race. The cost of the arms race was very great. The stockpiles of weapons that could kill everything on Earth, even if they were used by mistake, cost both sides money that should have been used in productive ways. The race was slowed by "arms control treaties," but it continued to weaken all the countries involved.

The Korean War. The first of the "proxy wars" was the Korean War between South Korea, aided by the United Nations forces led by the U.S., and North Korea, aided by Russia's communist ally, "Red" China. After three years of suffering (1950-1953), the war ended with no gain of land on either side.

The Vietnam War. Then came the long civil war in Vietnam and the rest of Southeast Asia. The U.S. was in direct combat from 1965 until 1973. The war poisoned the land and the lives of most of the people who fought and of those civilians who just lived through it. The United States left without winning, and the North Vietnamese eventually took over the South in 1975. But no one really won. The people of the whole region (particularly Vietnam, Laos, and Cambodia) were left an impoverished and brutalized world. Then the U.S. and the U.N. watched as a communist government in Cambodia killed millions of its own people.

Vietnam War Memorial: Three Soldiers

The Collapse of the U.S.S.R. The Cold War continued. The U.S. became involved in a number of other civil wars and struggles around the world, usually with support from the U.N. The U.S.S.R., in an attempt to gain control of a neighboring Islamic country, Afghanistan, took the side of a Marxist government against Islamic resistance in another civil war. The U.S. and U.N. didn't fight directly, but supported the anti-communist mujahideen. After ten years (1979-1989), the Russians finally withdrew without winning. The loss of the war, the cost of the arms race, a steep drop in oil income, and failed domestic reforms contributed to the gradual collapse of the Soviet government between 1985 and 1991 – the U.S.S.R. broke up into independent countries. America had survived the Cold War and was left the world's strongest military and economic "superpower." But there were costs.

Social Change. American history during the long Cold War was characterized by continuous social change brought about through public protest on various issues. Some major issues have been: the civil rights movement, aimed at gaining equality for African Americans; the women's liberation movement; protests against American involvement in the Vietnam War; the gay rights movement (for equal rights for homosexuals); various movements against both military and industrial uses of nuclear power; and most recently, a growing awareness of the pollution and destruction of the environment. Young people were often behind these movements, and they created a "counter culture" that influenced politics but also style, music, morality, and the American language.

The Rich-Poor Gap. During the twelve-year Ronald Reagan-George Bush administration, starting in the 1980s and increasing through the Bill Clinton and early George W. Bush years, the nation and the international economy enjoyed growth. Among other policies, the growth of free trade on a worldwide basis brought greater prosperity to many people. During the same time, however, the United States and other leading industrialized nations made little effort to solve the problem of increasing poverty. The "gap" between rich and poor nations and individuals continued to increase.

Terrorism. This problem stimulated social unrest and popular protests against global free trade and giant international corporations in many parts of the world. "America" became a symbol and focus for these protests. And widespread unhappiness over economic, political, social, and religious conditions stimulated the growth of terrorism. It occurred in many parts of the world. On 9/11/2001, terrorism finally struck the United States with the infamous attacks on New York's World Trade Towers and the Pentagon. The U.S. government responded with the invasion of Afghanistan and soon after that with the very controversial invasion of Iraq. By 2010, the war in Afghanistan had become the longest war in U.S. history.

The World Wide "Bubble." In 2007-2008 the era of prosperity ended. The world economy began the greatest collapse since the 1930s. In the U.S. there were many causes: the cost of the Middle Eastern wars; policies that stimulated growth by deregulating most industries; the Federal Goverment spending money without raising taxes, thus greatly increasing the national debt and spending borrowed money while cutting taxes for the richest Americans. The short-term bubble of prosperity this created was not sustainable. The crisis began with irresponsible mortages developed by unscrupulous international bankers. The international financial markets were now integrated and interdependent. The world-wide bubble burst.

Environmental Disasters. In recent years, scientists around the world have become more and more alarmed by to the effects of global warming brought on by increasing industrialization. International treaties were developed to begin to solve the problem, but the U.S. refused to sign them. Some U.S. politicians argued that accepting the "fiction" of global warming would hurt the U.S. economy. Then, as the world economy collapsed, there was a series of environmental disasters; some in the Middle East and Africa were caused by war and sabotage; many were the result of a lack of attention to safety regulations. When old, weak levees failed, Hurricane Katrina (2005) destroyed much of the city of New Orleans. Oil spills around the world indicated the need for stronger safety regulations; however, with the international demand for oil and other forms of energy growing, the U.S. continued to deregulate the energy industry.

A 2010 Oil spill at a British Petroleum deep-sea drilling site in the Gulf of Mexico caused an environmental disaster.

The Obama Administration. In 2008, the American people elected the first African-American President, Barack Obama, hoping that he would end the wars, restore world peace and prosperity, establish rational environmental policies, and rebuild an honest and fair government. Attempting to save the financial system and the automotive industry, Obama's administration temporarily followed the policy of the Bush administration and increased the debt. A complete collapse of the economy was avoided. This, however, was difficult and expensive. Working with a majority in Congress and against united Republican opposition, the Democrats passed changes in healthcare and health insurance, in financial regulation, and in education. Obama was re-elected in 2012. As promised he withdrew U.S. troops from Afghanistan and Iraq, but fighting continued in the Middle East. The U.S. economy recovered; unemployment and the deficit were reduced. However, in the U.S., as it is in most of the world, the need for reform and growth is great and progress is often blocked by partisan political struggles.

3.2 Four Noteworthy American Presidents

George Washington, 1732–1799

George Washington, who became the first U.S. president, was born in 1732 in Virginia, where his father was a prosperous planter. After serving heroically as commander in chief of the Continental Army in the American Revolution, he presided in 1787 over the convention that wrote the Constitution. Many leaders contributed to this process, but without Washington's stern and fair moral leadership, it was said the Constitution could not have been written. Washington was unanimously voted the first president in 1789 and was reelected in 1793. Setting the standard of the two-term presidency, he retired in 1798. He died at his home at Mount Vernon in 1799. All over the world today, it is common for national heroes to be called "the George Washington" of their country.

Abraham Lincoln, 1809–1865

Abraham Lincoln, the sixteenth U.S. president, was born in a log cabin to a Kentucky farm family who moved to Indiana when he was still very young. Later, he settled in Illinois, where he studied law on his own and served in the state legislature as a member of the Whig party. He was elected to the U.S. House of Representatives in 1847 and in 1858 ran unsuccessfully for the U.S. Senate against Stephen A. Douglas. The Lincoln–Douglas debates brought Lincoln public attention for his antislavery positions, and in 1860 he became the presidential nominee of the new Republican

Party. His election prompted the Southern states to secede from the Union and form the Confederacy. During the civil war that followed (1861–1865), Lincoln issued the Emancipation Proclamation, which defined the war as a crusade against slavery. His well-known Gettysburg Address (1863) further defined the war as the struggle for preservation of "government of the people, by the people, for the people." In 1865, immediately after the Union victory, Lincoln was assassinated by John Wilkes Booth, a Southern sympathizer enraged because the Confederacy had lost.

Franklin Delano Roosevelt, 1882–1945

Franklin Delano Roosevelt, the thirty-second U.S. president, was born in Hyde Park, New York, into the same family that had produced his distant cousin President Theodore Roosevelt and his own wife, Eleanor Roosevelt. Despite an attack of polio in 1921 that left him unable to walk without assistance, he ran successfully for governor of New York and served from 1929 to 1933. He easily defeated Republican Herbert Hoover in 1932, during the Great Depression, and launched an ambitious economic and social program that he called the "New Deal," designed to put people to work, get the economy moving, and create hope. Although the Depression did not end until the onset of World War II, Roosevelt's efforts earned him the loyalty of working people; he was reelected by a landslide vote in 1936 and won third and fourth terms, as well, in 1940 and 1944. Having seen the country through World War II, Roosevelt died of a stroke less than four weeks before the German surrender in 1945. He continues to be regarded as one of the three or four greatest American presidents.

John Fitzgerald Kennedy, 1917–1963

John F. Kennedy, the thirty-fifth U.S. president, was born in Brookline, Massachusetts, of Irish-American descent. Wounded in World War II, he entered politics after the war and was elected as a Democrat to the U.S. House of Representatives (1947–1953) and then the Senate (1953–1961). In 1960 he was elected U.S. president, the first Catholic and, at age 43, the youngest man to win that office. He is remembered for his active support of desegregation, for his "New Frontier" social programs, for establishing the Peace Corps, and for inspiring the space program. In 1962 he brought the country to the brink of nuclear war in the Cuban missile crisis, but the following year he secured a nuclear test ban treaty with the USSR. In November of that year, his presidency was cut short when he was assassinated in Dallas, Texas.

3.3 *Three Noteworthy Americans*

In 1963, one year before he was awarded the Nobel Peace Prize and five years before he was assassinated at the age of 39, civil rights leader Martin Luther King, Jr., gave a speech to a Peace March at the Lincoln Memorial in Washington, D.C. His "I Have a Dream" speech gave a new, deep meaning to the expression "the American Dream." King was a modern prophet, and in his speech, he referred to the words of two earlier American prophets, Thomas Jefferson, who wrote the *Declaration of Independence* and later was the third U.S. president, and Abraham Lincoln, the sixteenth president, who 87 years after the *Declaration* gave an address dedicating the new Civil War cemetery at Gettysburg, Pennsylvania.

Thomas Jefferson, from the *Declaration of Independence, 1776*

We hold these Truths to be self-evident, that all Men are created equal, that they are endowed by their Creator with certain unalienable Rights, that among these are Life, Liberty, and the Pursuit of Happiness – That to secure these Rights, Governments are instituted among Men, deriving their just Powers from the Consent of the Governed.

Abraham Lincoln's *Gettysburg Address, 1863*

Fourscore* and seven years ago our fathers brought forth on this continent a new nation, conceived in liberty and dedicated to the proposition that all men are created equal.

Now we are engaged in a great civil war, testing whether that nation or any nation so conceived and so dedicated, can long endure. We are met on a great battlefield of that war. We have come to dedicate a portion of that field as a final resting place for those who here gave their lives that that nation might live. It is altogether fitting and proper that we should do this.

But, in a larger sense, we cannot dedicate – we cannot consecrate – we cannot hallow this ground. The brave men, living and dead, who struggled here, have consecrated it, far above our poor power to add or to detract. The world will little note nor long remember what we say here, but it can never forget what they did here. It is for us the living, rather, to be here dedicated to the great task remaining before us – that from these honored dead we take increased devotion – that we here highly resolve that these dead shall not have died in vain – that this nation, under God, shall have a new birth of freedom – and that government of the people, by the people, for the people, shall not perish from the earth.

* A "score" of years means twenty years.

Martin Luther King, Jr., from *I Have a Dream*, 1963

Fivescore years ago, a great American, in whose symbolic shadow we stand, signed the Emancipation Proclamation. This momentous decree came as a great beacon of hope to millions of Negro slaves who had been seared in the flames of withering injustice. It came as a joyous daybreak to end the long night of captivity. But one hundred years later, we must face the tragic fact that the Negro is still not free...

I say to you today, my friends, that in spite of difficulties and frustrations of the moment I still have a dream. It is a dream deeply rooted in the American Dream.

I have a dream that one day this nation will rise up and live out the true meaning of its creed: "We hold these truths to be self-evident; that all men are created equal."

I have a dream that one day on the red hills of Georgia the sons of former slaves and the sons of former slave-owners will be able to sit down together at the table of brotherhood.

I have a dream that one day even the state of Mississippi, a desert state sweltering with the heat of injustice and oppression, will be transformed into an oasis of freedom and justice.

I have a dream that my four little children will one day live in a nation where they will not be judged by the color of their skin but by the content of their character....

When we let freedom ring, when we let it ring from every village and every hamlet, from every state and every city, we will be able to speed up that day when all God's children, black men and white men, Jews and Gentiles, Protestants and Catholics, will be able to join hands and sing in the words of the old Negro spiritual, "Free at last! Free at last! Thank God almighty, we are free at last!"

3.4 Political Map

On the next page (page 53) you will find a map of the 50 states. The key to the map is on page 54. Each state is also listed with its postal abbreviation.

Washington, D.C. (District of Columbia) is between the states of Maryland and Virginia. It is a federal district and does not belong to any state.

Puerto Rico and the United States Virgin Islands are not states, but they are associated with the United States, as are the Pacific Islands of Guam (GU), American Samoa (AS), and the Northern Marianas (MP).

The United States

1	ME	Maine	28	AZ	Arizona
2	VT	Vermont	29	CA	California
3	NH	New Hampshire	30	NV	Nevada
4	MA	Massachusetts	31	OR	Oregon
5	RI	Rhode Island	32	WA	Washington
6	CT	Connecticut	33	ID	Idaho
7	NY	New York	34	UT	Utah
8	PA	Pennsylvania	35	MT	Montana
9	WV	West Virginia	36	WY	Wyoming
10	VA	Virginia	37	CO	Colorado
11	NJ	New Jersey	38	ND	North Dakota
12	DE	Delaware	39	SD	South Dakota
13	MD	Maryland	40	NE	Nebraska
14	MI	Michigan	41	KS	Kansas
15	IN	Indiana	42	OK	Oklahoma
16	OH	Ohio	43	MN	Minnesota
17	KY	Kentucky	44	IA	Iowa
18	TN	Tennessee	45	IL	Illinois
19	NC	North Carolina	46	MO	Missouri
20	SC	South Carolina	47	AR	Arkansas
21	GA	Georgia	48	WI	Wisconsin
22	AL	Alabama	49	HI	Hawaii
23	FL	Florida	50	AK	Alaska
24	MS	Mississippi	51	PR	Puerto Rico
25	LA	Louisiana	52	VI	Virgin Islands
26	TX	Texas	53	DC	District of Columbia
27	NM	New Mexico			

3.5 Land and People

The United States is the fourth largest country in the world in area and the third in population. Its land and climate vary from region to region, and its peoples have come from all of the cultures of the world.

Regions. There are seven regions in the United States, not including Alaska (AK) and Hawaii (Hl). They are listed below. The 48 states listed below are sometimes called the continental or contiguous (touching) states. In Alaska they are called the "lower 48," and in Hawaii people call them "the mainland."

New England		*Midwest*	
CT	NH	IL	MO
MA	RI	IN	NE
ME	VT	IA	ND
		KS	OH
Mid-Atlantic		MI	SD
DE	NY	MN	WI
MD	PA		
NJ		*Rocky Mountains*	
		CO	NV
South		ID	UT
AL	MS	MT	WY
AR	NC		
FL	SC	*Southwest*	
GA	TN	AZ	OK
KY	VA	NM	TX
LA	WV		
		Pacific or West Coast	
		CA	WA
		OR	

Note: The state names abbreviated in the list above are given with their abbreviations on page 52. For many states there are two abbreviations for the state name. For example, **Mississippi** can be **MS** or **Miss.** The Post Office encourages the use of the MS form (two capital letters without punctuation).

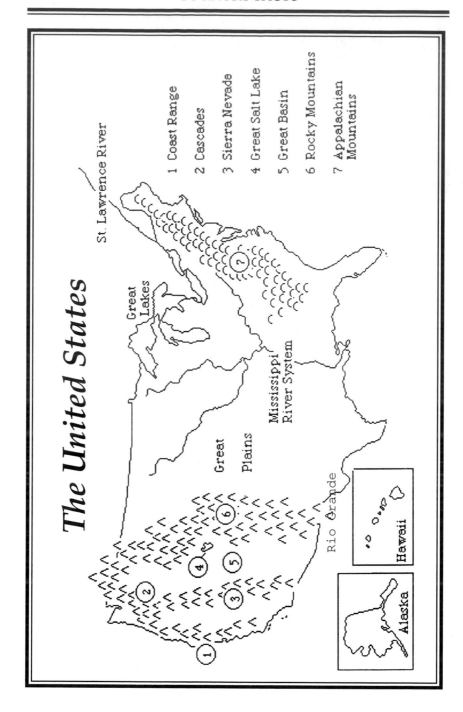

The United States

St. Lawrence River

Great Lakes

Mississippi River System

Great Plains

Rio Grande

Alaska

Hawaii

1 Coast Range
2 Cascades
3 Sierra Nevada
4 Great Salt Lake
5 Great Basin
6 Rocky Mountains
7 Appalachian Mountains

Land. The United States has an area of 9,371,781 square kilometers. Alaska is the largest state. It is about the same size as Portugal, Spain, France, and Germany together. Alaska is very mountainous. The highest mountain is Denali, which is 6,914 meters high – the highest in North America.

Hawaii is a group of islands in the Pacific Ocean, 3,857 kilometers from California. The islands are actually the tops of volcanoes. Hawaii is one of the smallest states (16,760 square kilometers). It is a little smaller than Kuwait.

The other 48 states stretch across the North American continent for about 4,800 kilometers from the Atlantic to the Pacific. There is a wide variety of land forms; the major features are shown on the map on the facing page. Along the Atlantic Coast the land is flat. Inland from the coast there is a low range of mountains, the Appalachian Mountains. The highest point is Mount Mitchell in North Carolina (2,037 meters).

Rivers. In the middle of the continent are two large river systems, the great Mississippi River, which flows south to the Gulf of Mexico, and the Great Lakes and the Saint Lawrence River which flow northeast through Canada to the Atlantic Ocean. The middle part of the country is generally flat, and toward the west, it is very open – from Texas north to the Dakotas this area is called the Great Plains.

Mountains. The west is mountainous. There are two main mountain systems: The Rocky Mountains and, nearer the Pacific, the Sierra Nevada and the Coast/Cascade Range. In between the moun tain ranges is a dry, semidesert area called the Great Basin. Great Salt Lake is in the middle of this basin. The highest mountain in the west is Mount Whitney (4,418 meters) in the Sierra Nevada of California.

Climate. The climate of the United States is temperate, with four distinct seasons. The northern half of the country usually has snow in the winter. The coldest months are December, January, and February, and the warmest are June, July, and August.

The coldest U.S. strates are Alaska, Montana, the Dakotas, Minnesota, Wisconsin, northern Michigan, northern New York, and northern New England. The hottest places are the Carolinas, Florida, Georgia, Alabama, Mississippi, Louisiana, Texas, New Mexico, and Arizona.

Southern Florida and Hawaii are sub-tropical. Southern California has a Mediterranean-type climate. The driest areas are southern California, Nevada, Utah, Arizona, New Mexico, and northern Alaska. The East is much wetter than the West, and the wettest areas are in the lower Mississippi basin.

Population. The population is estimated to be 316 million by the beginning of 2014, . 80.3% of the population lives in metropolitan areas (cities), 19.7% in rural areas (countryside). The largest state is California, with a population of 38 million. Six other states have populations of over 10 million. They are (highest to lowest) Texas, New York, Florida, Illinois, Pennsylvania, and Ohio. The four states with the smallest populations are Alaska, North Dakota, Vermont, and Wyoming. For more information, see the Appendix.

In recent years the U.S. population has shifted south and then west. Climate is one reason; economics is another. Industries and the people who work in them have moved from the so-called "rust belt" to the "sun belt." Nevada, Arizona, Georgia, the Carolinas, and Texas have grown much faster than such northern industrial states as New York, Pennsylvania, Ohio, Michigan, and Illinois. The populations of urban areas have grown faster than those of rural areas. At the same time, the populations of the urban areas have shifted from the "inner cities" to the suburbs, although this shift has slowed recently. Unlike cities in many parts of the world, American cities have centers troubled with poverty and crime, while the surrounding, more open areas are generally wealthier and have fewer social problems.

The **Largest Cities** are listed below according to the 2013 Census Bureau estimate. The metropolitan figures include the smaller cities and towns that are around the city itself.

City, State	City Population	Metropolitan Population
New York, NY	9,405,837	19,949,502
Los Angeles, CA	3,884,307	13,131,431
Chicago, IL	2,718,782	9,537,289
Houston, TX	2,195,914	6,313,158
Philadelphia, PA	1,553,165	6,034,678
Phoenix, AZ	1,513,367	4,398,762
San Antonio, TX	1,409,019	2,277,550
San Diego, CA	1,355,896	3,211,252
Dallas, TX	1,257,676	6,110,913
San Jose, CA	998,537	1,919,641

Language. American English is the dominant language spoken throughout the country. There are dialects in different regions (Northern, Midland, and Southern), but Americans usually do not have any difficulty understanding each other.

In some parts of the United States you will encounter large groups of people who use another language on a daily basis. Spanish is the first language for many people in New York City, Miami, the Southwest, and California. You will find people in northern New England and New York who speak Canadian French. Many Native Americans, including the native people of Alaska and Hawaii, have their own languages. Although most Americans are monolingual, in recent years bilingualism has become more common.

Ethnic Groups. There are many minority ethnic groups in the United States. The largest such group is Spanish-speaking people from Mexico, Puerto Rico, Cuba, and other countries. They are about 17.8% of the population. African Americans are about 13% of the population. Asian Americans are mainly Chinese, Japanese, and Indochinese. They represent about 5.6% of the U.S. population. Native Americans are a little less than one percent of the total.

3.4 Government

Government operates on three levels in the United States: national, state, and local. The Constitution of the United States outlines the basic principles on which the government is founded, and it describes the powers that belong to federal and state governments.

The Federal Government makes and enforces laws, collects taxes, provides services, and protects the people while working toward national and international security. There are three branches of federal government: executive, legislative, and judicial.

The Executive Branch is made up of the President, executive departments, and independent agencies. The President of the United States is responsible for enforcing laws, choosing high government officials, commanding the army, conducting foreign affairs, and recommending laws to Congress. The executive departments are responsible for the administration of the federal government. There are 15 departments: State, Treasury, Defense, Justice, Interior, Agriculture, Commerce, Labor, Health and Human Services, Homeland Security, Housing and Urban Development, Transportation, Energy, Education, and Veterans Affairs. The independent agencies help implement and regulate laws. They operate in fields such as nuclear energy, interstate commerce, small business, communications, etc.

The Legislative Branch of the United States government includes Congress (which consists of the Senate and the House of Representatives) and a number of administrative agencies. Congress makes and changes laws, establishes federal taxes, and decides on funds for operating the federal government. The Senate has 100 members, two from each state. The House of Representatives has 435 members, who are divided among the states according to the number of people living in each state. Distribution of seats in the House is changed every ten years to keep up to date with the country's current population as determined by the census. The largest state, California, has 55 representatives. The seven smallest states have one representative each. The District of Columbia has one representative and no senators.

The Judicial Branch of the government consists of the Supreme Court, the highest court in the country. There are nine justices on the Supreme Court. They are appointed by the President. Federal district courts are located throughout the nation. There are also 11 federal appeals courts, which are above the district courts. Federal courts decide cases that involve federal laws and the Constitution.

Political Parties. There are two major political parties in the United States: Democrat and Republican. Most members of government come from one of these two parties, although several minor parties also exist.

National Elections. Every two years on the first Tuesday in November, national, state, and local elections are held. Representatives to Congress are elected every two years, the President and Vice-President are elected every four years, and Senators are elected every six years. The next presidential election is scheduled for 2016. A citizen must be at least 18 years old to vote. (See the Appendix for additional information.)

State Governments are similar to the national government. The executive officer is called the governor, and each state has a legislature and a judicial system. State government is important in controlling roads, vehicles and drivers, social welfare programs, public universities, prisons, banking, tourism, and utilities such as electric companies.

Local Government can be administered at the county, city, town, or village level. Each state is divided into counties. Counties are important in some states, and less important in others. The best known county officer is the head of the county police, the sheriff. The highest political officer in a city is called the mayor.

The mayor usually works with a small executive advisory group called the city council or aldermen. Each city has its own police force. Town government is similar to city government, but it is smaller and is usually administered by a small committee of community leaders. Cities and towns are responsible for public schools, local streets and roads, water and sewer, and services such as waste collection, public transportation, public libraries, and recreational facilities. (Incidentally, the public library is a good place to visit. You can learn a lot about the town and meet local people there.)

3.7 Free Enterprise

Free Enterprise. The economy of the United States is based on free enterprise. In such a system, individual people and companies are free to make their own economic decisions. They own the raw materials and machinery needed to make their product, and they decide how to market their product in order to make a profit. The federal government is involved in the system by regulating business in certain ways. For instance, it establishes antitrust laws to prevent one company from controlling an entire industry, and laws to prevent environmental pollution.

Natural Resources. The United States has many natural resources: fuels for energy such as coal, petroleum, and natural gas; rich soil for agriculture; water for agriculture and industry; forests that provide wood for building and paper; and both freshwater and ocean fish.

Service and Manufacturing. Service is the economic activity that employs the greatest number of Americans. The service economy is often contrasted to manufacturing, which has been in decline for years as industries have moved the production of products to other countries where labor is less expensive. Economists and politicians debate whether the shift from manufacturing to service makes the U.S. stronger or weaker. These changes in the economy of a company or the nation are called "restructuring."

3.8 Religion

Religious Freedom. The Constitution of the United States specifically forbids the establishment of a state religion. The First Amendment guarantees freedom of religion for every citizen of the nation. This freedom is one reason that many people have immigrated. As a result, there are many different religions in the U.S. Of the people who say that they are religious, approximately 78% are Christian, 4.7 belong to other organized religious groups, and the rest aren't members of a group. Of the Christians, 51% are Protestant (Baptist, United Methodist, Presbyterian, Lutheran, and Episcopalian, etc.), 24% are Roman Catholic, 2% are Mormon, and .6% belong to Eastern Orthodox Churches. 4.7% of Americans identify with other religions. 1.7% are Jewish, .7% are Buddhist, .6% are Muslim, and .4% are Hindu.

Although there are a variety of religious groups in the United States, Christian traditions have influenced the country the most. All offices are closed on Sundays, and many holidays are based on Christian tradition (see section 2.14).

3.9 Education

Education in the United States is based on the belief that learning how to think for oneself through research and problem-solving skills is more important than learning facts.

Public, Parochial, and Private Schools. Education is guaranteed to all children from the age of 5 through 18 in the public school system. Public schools are funded with money from taxes, so parents do not pay a specific additional charge when their children attend a public school. Other types of schools are parochial and private schools. Parochial schools are funded by religious denominations, and parents with children in those schools pay tuition. Private schools are self-supporting and are therefore the most expensive.

Pre-school. Americans often begin their education at a public or private nursery school when they are 2, 3, or 4 years old. Nursery schools give children a chance to learn to play with other children and to begin learning skills that will help them in school.

Kindergarten and Elementary School. At five, most students go to local public schools for a year of kindergarten, followed by elementary school (sometimes called grade school, grammar school, or primary school). They are required by law to start in first grade at age 6.

Middle and High School. After elementary school, students attend middle school or junior high school and then high school. In all, they spend 12 years in elementary, middle school, and high school (also called secondary school). These schools are controlled by locally elected school boards.

Higher Education. After high school, there are a number of different types of institutions that offer higher education. Community colleges provide two years of higher education. State colleges and universities provide the four years of education needed to receive a bachelor's degree; these two- and four-year programs are called undergraduate education. The universities also have graduate schools that offer additional education for a master's degree and/or a doctorate. Fees vary from state to state. In addition to tax-supported community and state (public) institutions, there are also many private colleges and universities. They are usually more expensive than public institutions.

3.8 The Arts

In general, the arts in America have been influenced by three traditions: European, Native American, and African. The unique American experience of exploring and developing a new continent has also influenced the arts.

Native American Influence. The decorative traditions of Native American art are still seen in many designs, especially in weaving and pottery. These traditions existed before the arrival of European explorers. The American Southwest is the contemporary center of this tradition.

European Influence. Many settlers from Europe arrived during the seventeenth and eighteenth centuries. They brought their artistic traditions with them. Many artists and craftsmen, however, produced distinctive American art forms that are called Colonial (early 1600s to late 1700s) and Federalist (late 1700s to early 1800s). Especially well known are the furniture and household furnishings of these times. Americans are also very proud of the architecture of this period. Many buildings have been preserved and restored. The U.S. government now protects over 2,500 national historic landmarks, and many other government and private organizations protect other architectural and historic sites. In some places villages have been restored or rebuilt. Some of the best known are Williamsburg in Virginia, Sturbridge Village and Plymouth Plantation in Massachusetts, and Strawbery Banke in New Hampshire. One famous house in Boston, Massachusetts, is the home of Paul Revere, a hero of the Revolution and a great silversmith.

American Literature. During the nineteenth century, American literature began speaking in a voice different from English literature. The American wilderness and frontier, along with American ideas of freedom and independence, contributed in important ways to writers who are still well known. James Fenimore Cooper was America's first popular novelist. He wrote novels about the frontier, such as *The Last of the Mohicans*. Ralph Waldo Emerson and Henry David Thoreau were essayists who celebrated American self-reliance and independent thinking. Herman Melville's *Moby Dick* stands as one of the classics of world literature. One of it themes is a battle of man against nature – the hunt for a great white whale. Walt Whitman became America's first great poet, with the notion of democracy as one of his central themes. In 1884, Mark Twain published his masterpiece, *Huckleberry Finn*, perhaps the most important American novel ever written. But the most powerful novel of the nineteenth century was *Uncle Tom's Cabin*, written by Harriet Beecher Stowe in 1852. It brought international attention to the evils of slavery, and it is often called one of the causes of the American Civil War.

In the fields of **painting and sculpture**, American artists tended to work within the European tradition. Some artists produced work with distinctly American themes. Thomas Cole was the first important landscape painter in the United States. He founded the

Hudson River School (1820–1850). Artists in this school portrayed American forests, rivers, and mountains in romantic scenes. In the twentieth century, a group of regional painters, sometimes called anti-modernists, tried to portray the strength and energy of rural America. Thomas Hart Benton of Missouri was one of the most successful artists of the 1930s.

Art Museums. There are over 7,000 art museums in the United States. Many of these museums have special collections of American art. The most important collections can be seen in the Los Angeles County Museum, the Chicago Art Institute, the Butler Institute in Youngstown, Ohio, the Philadelphia Museum of Art, the Boston Museum of Fine Arts, the Smithsonian Institution in Washington, D.C., and, in New York City, the Metropolitan Museum of Art, the Museum of Modern Art, and the Whitney Museum of American Art.

Louis Armstrong
(1901-1971)
– aka Satchmo

Music and the African American Influence. The African American experience has been the most important influence on music in America. In the nineteenth century, African Americans developed religious songs called spirituals. These choral songs, based on African call-and-response patterns, led to a variety of musical forms, from gospel music to blues and jazz. The jazz of African Americans is a unique contribution to the music of the contemporary world, from pop to rock to classical music.

The Cinema and Skyscraper. Throughout the twentieth century, American writers, musicians, dancers, painters, sculptors, craftsmen, and architects continued to find ways to express both the diversity and the unity of the American experience. Two art forms stand out among others: the cinema and the skyscraper. The cinema, popularly called the movies, along with its cousin, television, dominates mass entertainment worldwide. The skyscraper dominates the skyline of America's cities as a symbol of America as the most powerful country in the world. As a symbol, the skyscrapers of the World Trade Center in New York City became the target of terrorism.

3.11 Technology and Change

The United States has been profoundly shaped and changed by technological developments, as has the rest of the world.

The Railroad. In the 19th century, the development of the railroad was a significant factor in the development of the continent. In 1869, the east and west coasts were linked by an intercontinental railway. From that time on, more and more Americans looked to the "Golden West" as a new frontier. The lives of the Native Americans of the West were changed forever.

Electrification. Late in the 19th century, Thomas Edison invented the light bulb. The day no longer ended with sunset, and the resulting electrification of the country intensified the great industrial revolution of the 19th century. The American family, and especially American women, began to enjoy dozens of labor-saving devices such as the electric refrigerator and the dishwasher.

The Telephone. In 1876 Alexander Graham Bell invented the telephone, and instant communication over distance became part of everyday life in the 20th century. The cell phone of the 21st century expands telephone usage to anywhere, any time.

The Auto and the Airplane. Possibly the most profound development of the 20th century was Henry Ford's mass production of the **automobile** in 1908. This caused the roads of America to be developed, culminating in the Interstate Highway System. Cities changed as suburbs grew. The trucking industry replaced the railroad in importance. The auto industry of Detroit became a significant part of the American economy. And the people of America became a population on wheels, moving freely to new jobs, homes, and communities. Soon after the auto mobile came **aviation,** launched by the Wright Brothers in 1903. The industry took off after WWI in the 1920s. Eventually, every city in the country could be reached in just a few hours.

Nuclear and Alternative Power. On the international scene, the development of nuclear weapons, for better or worse, has certainly dominated world politics and has made the United States a world superpower. In the domestic scene, nuclear energy plants became more and more common, but not without controversy. Accidents at nuclear power stations like Chernobyl (1986) in Ukraine and Fukushima (2011) in Japan, countries around the world have increasingly turned to wind, sun, and water power as alternatives to fossil fuels and nuclear energy for power.

Television. Beginning in the 1950s, the development of television ("TV") caused a great change in the way families lived their daily lives. The TV also changed the way individuals viewed the world. Debate over the positive and negative impacts of TV is a discussion that is still going on.

Space Exploration. Many technological innovations have grown out of America's and other countries' exploration of space. Satellites monitor the weather, make worldwide communication possible. GPS (Global Positioning System) has allowed us to track ships at sea, migrating bird and animals, travelers, and children at play. The space shuttles helped launch hundreds of these satellites, including space telescopes that have given us a new understanding of space, time, and the physical universe. The space shuttle program ended in 2011. America, Russia, and their allies have built have built a space station that is stimulating new technologies for the future benefit of people all over the earth.

The Computer and the Internet. Since the last decades of the 20th Century, the computer and the Internet have revolutionized and integrated culture, commerce, and communication around the world for businesses, families, and individuals. Within one generation, the telephone, mails, and television have spread to world-wide use of devices from super-computers to computer watches. Sending personal messages and using social media – the whole digital revolution has now transformed everyone's life.

Appendix: The 50 States

This list of the 50 states and the federal District of Columbia emphasizes the connection between politics and population. Population figures are based on the 2013 Census Bureau estimates (rounded to the nearest 100). A new national census will be taken in 2020. A census is taken every ten years and has been since 1790.

Electoral votes are used for presidential elections only. The candidate who gets the most votes in a state wins all the electoral votes of that state. The electoral vote is based on the number of senators and representatives from that state. Each state has two senators. The number of representatives is determined by the population of the state.

For example, as a result of the 2010 census, California, with the largest population, has 53 representatives and two senators and thus 55 electoral votes.

(R) signifies Republican Party, (D) stands for Democratic Party, and (I) means Independent.

1. **California**. Capital: Sacramento
Population: 38,332,500
Electoral Votes: 55
2012 vote: Obama
Senators: Feinstein (D), Boxer (D)

2. **Texas**. Capital: Austin
Population: 26,448,200
Electoral Votes: 38
2012 vote: Romney
Senators: Cruz (R), Cornyn (R)

3. **New York**. Capital: Albany
Population: 19,651,100
Electoral Votes: 29
2012 vote: Obama
Senators: Gillebrand (D), Schumer (D)

4. **Florida**. Capital: Tallahassee
Population: 19,552,900
Electoral Votes: 29
2012 vote: Obama
Senators: Nelson (D), Rubio (R)

5. **Illinois**. Capital: Springfield
Population: 12,882,100
Electoral Votes: 20
2012 vote: Obama
Senators: Durbin (D), Kirk (R)

6. **Pennsylvania**. Capital: Harrisburg
Population: 12,773,800
Electoral Votes: 20
2012 vote: Obama
Senators: Casey (D), Toomey (R)

7. Ohio. Capital: Columbus
Population: 11,570,800
Electoral Votes: 18
2012 vote: Obama
Senators: Brown (D), Portman (R)

8. Georgia. Capital: Atlanta
Population: 9,992,200
Electoral Votes: 16
2012 vote: Romney
Senators: Perdue (R), Isakson (R)

9. Michigan. Capital: Lansing
Population: 9,895,600
Electoral Votes: 16
2012 vote: Obama
Senators: Stabenow (D), Peters (D)

10. North Carolina. Capital: Raleigh
Population: 9,848,100
Electoral Votes: 15
2012 vote: Romney
Senators: Tillis (R), Burr (R)

11. New Jersey. Capital: Trenton
Population: 8,899,300
Electoral Votes: 14
2012 vote: Obama
Senators: Menendez (D), Booker (D)

12. Virginia. Capital: Richmond
Population: 8,260,400
Electoral Votes: 13
2012 vote: Obama
Senators: Kaine (D), Warner (D)

13. Washington. Capital: Olympia
Population: 6,971,400
Electoral Votes: 12
2012 vote: Obama
Senators: Cantwell (D), Murray (D)

14. Massachusetts. Capital: Boston
Population: 6,692,800
Electoral Votes: 11
2012 vote: Obama
Senators: Markey (D), Warren (D)

15. Arizona. Capital: Phoenix
Population: 6,626,600
Electoral Votes: 11
2012 vote: Romney
Senators: Flake (R), McCain (R)

16. Indiana. Capital: Indianapolis
Population: 6,570,900
Electoral Votes: 11
2012 vote: Romney
Senators: Coats (R), Donnelly (D)

17. Tennessee. Capital: Nashville
Population: 6,496,000
Electoral Votes: 11
2012 vote: Romney
Senators: Corker (R), Alexander (R)

18. Missouri. Capital: Jefferson City
Population: 6,044,200
Electoral Votes: 10
2012 vote: Romney
Senators: McCaskill (D), Blunt (R)

19. Maryland. Capital: Annapolis
Population: 5,928,800
Electoral Votes: 10
2012 vote: Obama
Senators: Cardin (D), Mikulski (D)

20. Wisconsin. Capital: Madison
Population: 5,742,700
Electoral Votes: 10
2012 vote: Obama
Senators: Baldwin (D), Johnson (R)

21. **Minnesota**. Capital: St. Paul
Population: 5,420,400
Electoral Votes: 10
2012 vote: Obama
Senators: Klobacher (D), Franken (D)

22. **Colorado**. Capital: Denver
Population: 5,268,400
Electoral Votes: 9
2012 vote: Obama
Senators: Gardner (R), Bennet (D)

23. **Alabama**. Capital: Montgomery
Population: 4,833,700
Electoral Votes: 9
2012 vote: Romney
Senators: Sessions (R), Shelby (R)

24. **South Carolina**. Capital: Columbia
Population: 4,774,800
Electoral Votes: 9
2012 vote: Romney
Senators: Graham (R), Scott (R)

25. **Louisiana**. Capital: Baton Rouge
Population: 4,625,500
Electoral Votes: 8
2012 vote: Romney
Senators: Cassidy (R), Vitter (R)

26. **Kentucky**. Capital: Frankfort
Population: 4,395,300
Electoral Votes: 8
2012 vote: Romney
Senators: McConnell (R), Rand (R)

27. **Oregon**. Capital: Salem
Population: 3,930,100
Electoral Votes: 7
2012 vote: Obama
Senators: Merkley (D), Wyden (D)

28. **Oklahoma**. Capital: Oklahoma City
Population: 3,850,600
Electoral Votes: 7
2012 vote: Romney
Senators: Inhofe (R), Coburn (R)

29. **Connecticut**. Capital: Hartford
Population: 3,596,100
Electoral Votes: 7
2012 vote: Obama
Senators: Blumenthal (D), Murphy (D)

30. **Iowa**. Capital: Des Moines
Population: 3,080,400
Electoral Votes: 6
2012 vote: Obama
Senators: Ernst (R), Grassley (R)

31. **Mississippi**. Capital: Jackson
Population: 2,991,200
Electoral Votes: 6
2012 vote: Romney
Senators: Wicker (R), Cochran (R)

32. **Arkansas**. Capital: Little Rock
Population: 2,959,400
Electoral Votes: 6
2012 vote: Romney
Senators: Cotton (R), Boozmen (R)

33. **Utah**. Capital: Salt Lake City
Population: 2,900,900
Electoral Votes: 6
2012 vote: Romney
Senators: Hatch (R), Lee (R)

34. **Kansas**. Capital: Topeka
Population: 2,894,000
Electoral Votes: 6
2012 vote: Romney
Senators: Roberts (R), Moran (R)

35. **Nevada**. Capital: Carson City
Population: 2,790,100
Electoral Votes: 6
2012 vote: Obama
Senators: Heller (R), Reid (D)

36. **New Mexico**. Capital: Santa Fe
Population: 2,085,300
Electoral Votes: 5
2012 vote: Obama
Senators: Heinrich (D), Udall (D)

37. **Nebraska**. Capital: Lincoln
Population: 1,868,500
Electoral Votes: 5
2012 vote: Romney
Senators: Fischer (R), Sasse (R)

38. **West Virginia**. Capital: Charleston
Population: 1,854,300
Electoral Votes: 5
2012 vote: Romney
Senators: Manchin (D), Capito (R)

39. **Idaho**. Capital: Boise
Population: 1,612,100
Electoral Votes: 4
2012 vote: Romney
Senators: Risch (R), Crapo (R)

40. **Hawaii**. Capital: Honolulu
Population: 1,404,100
Electoral Votes: 4
2012 vote: Obama
Senators: Hirono (D), Schatz (D)

41. **Maine**. Capital: Augusta
Population: 1,328,300
Electoral Votes: 4
2012 vote: Obama
Senators: King (I), Collins (R)

42. **New Hampshire**. Capital: Concord
Population: 1,323,500
Electoral Votes: 4
2012 vote: Obama
Senators: Shaheen (D), Ayotte (R)

43. **Rhode Island**. Capital: Providence
Population: 1,051,500
Electoral Votes: 4
2012 vote: Obama
Senators: Whitehouse (D), Reed (D)

44. **Montana**. Capital: Helena
Population: 1,015,200
Electoral Votes: 3
2012 vote: Romney
Senators: Tester (D), Daines (R)

45. **Delaware**. Capital: Dover
Population: 925,800
Electoral Votes: 3
2012 vote: Obama
Senators: Coons (D), Carper (D)

46. **South Dakota**. Capital: Pierre
Population: 844,900
Electoral Votes: 3
2012 vote: Romney
Senators: Rounds (R), Thune (R)

47. **Alaska**. Capital: Juneau
Population: 735,100
Electoral Votes: 3
2012 vote: Romney
Senators: Sullivan (R), Murkowski (R)

48. **North Dakota**. Capital: Bismarck
Population: 723,500
Electoral Votes: 3
2012 vote: Romney
Senators: Heitkamp (D), Hoeven (R)

49. **Vermont**. Capital: Montpelier
Population: 626,600
Electoral Votes: 3
2012 vote: Obama
Senators: Sanders (I), Leahy (D)

50. **Wyoming**. Capital: Cheyenne
Population: 528,700
Electoral Votes: 3
2012 vote: Romney
Senators: Barrasso (R), Enzi (R)

District of Columbia. (USA Capital)
Population: 646,500
Electoral Votes: 3
2012 vote: Obama

Also Available from Pro Lingua Associates

Cultural Differences: Read, Discuss, and Write
A content-based college/university preparation course introducing
and giving practice in using a wide range of academic skills.
The content is focused on a neglected area of language-culture
studies: the conflicts that can occur when learners don't really
understand each other's language and culture.

Teaching in the United States
A Guide for International Educators
by Julie Damron, Ph.D.

American Holidays
Exploring Traditions, Customs, and Backgrounds, BOOK, CD
by Barbara Klebanow and Sara Fischer

All Around America
The Time Traveler's Talk Show
SCRIPTS, WORKBOOK, 2 CDS
by Anne Siebert and Raymond C. Clark

Legends: 52 People Who Made a Difference, BOOK, CD
A Graded Reader on American History
by Michael Ryall

Celebrating American Heroes, BOOK, CD
13 plays for Students of English
by Anne Siebert

Heroes from American History
A Content-Based Reader – 16 Biographies
by Anne Siebert and Raymond C. Clark

Pearls of Wisdom
African and Caribbean Folktales
STUDENT TEXT, WORKBOOK, 2 CDS
by Raouf Mama and Mary Romney

Story Cards
North American Indian Tales
by Susannah J. Clark